# JILL GORDON'S
## TAPESTRY COLLECTION

# JILL GORDON'S
# TAPESTRY COLLECTION

MEREHURST

NOTE: *For all designs, 1 skein of yarn in each colour listed is sufficient, unless otherwise indicated by a number in brackets after the relevant yarn.*

First published in 1997 by
Merehurst Limited, Ferry House,
51-57 Lacy Road, Putney,
London SW15 1PR

ISBN 1-85391-636-6

Edited by Heather Dewhurst
Designed by Janet James
Photography by Michelle Garrett
Charts by Ethan Danielson,
with assistance from Chartworks Limited

Colour separation by Bright Arts (HK) Limited

Printed by Olivotto, Italy

# CONTENTS

# INTRODUCTION

What inspired me to write this book? The answer is that when I had finished the designs for *The Tapestry Book*, it left me with even more ideas for unusual subjects that I wanted to translate into needlepoint designs, so the solution was to produce another book. The feedback I received from *The Tapestry Book* was that stitchers were thrilled to have more and more unusual subjects to stitch and that, although some people loved the traditional subjects and typically more sombre colours of needlepoints of the past, so many more were excited by new ideas and brilliant colours.

Now, after completing the designs for the *Tapestry Collection*, I am left with the feeling of wanting to do even more on each subject. It seems that designing is self-perpetuating – the more you design, the more you want to design. And as I have many more ideas than there are hours to stitch, this state of affairs will probably continue and I will never manage to stitch them all!

If I am ever asked to enlarge upon why I feel compelled to design, stitch and paint, I would say that we all have a sense of beauty locked away inside us and once we start to express this in some kind of material form, whether by creating paintings or needlepoints, then we are almost driven in our desire to make more and more beautiful or worthwhile creations. And, of course, each painting or needlepoint never seems quite to match up to our vision, so we try again, or else the completion of an idea gives rise to several others and these multiply into even more, so that it is a never-ending cycle of mostly pleasure and learning.

I am frequently asked what it is that inspires me. My immediate answer is 'everything', which is true in the sense that I am always looking at my surroundings, wherever I am, and turning them into drawings, storing ideas from them or just revelling in their beauty. Until I met Kaffe Fassett, I thought that I was odd because I found everything around me

interesting subject matter, even sometimes in its ugliness. Now it is fairly common to see photographs of beautiful clothes or knitwear set against peeling paintwork or crumbling stones, but I think Kaffe spearheaded this. It was a joyous revelation to me to go for a walk (or sometimes a run!) around dingy backstreets with Kaffe back in the 1970s, and listen to him enthusing about every little detail of texture and colour we passed – whether it was moss-covered walls, speckled roof tiles or simply glistening puddles.

Although I have an obsessive interest in old china, carpets, scarves, furniture and anything decorative, in the collection of designs for this book I have worked mostly from nature, which I find to be an endless source of inspiration. Perhaps it is because there are already many designers doing wonderful things with old patterns and decorative art that I have been drawn to using nature, or perhaps it is the challenge of trying to depict living creatures realistically in wool.

Certainly a great influence on my work is where I live, tucked away in a small valley fold just above the snow line, and just inside the Peak National Park. In the winter, we are often completely cut off as the lane from the house to the road is impassable as soon as there is any ice or snow. I do not own a four-wheel drive vehicle which would get me out in most weathers but being snowbound is a welcome excuse not to be able to go anywhere at all. The house is completely surrounded by beauty – I only wish that I could have more time to sit and contemplate it. The countryside around the house is very open and generally a rather windswept part of the world, but I am fortunate enough to have huge, ancient beech and horse chestnut trees near the house, which attract owls in great numbers. There is a stream nearby, which occasionally turns into a roaring torrent and can become impassable, but it does mean that we have grey herons and kingfishers frequently visiting. The grey herons are very shy but sometimes I am lucky enough to see them before I make a noise; I watch them as they stand still on one leg, or wade up the stream looking for food.

At the back of the house the land rises steeply, opening out into rough grassland which is a haven for skylarks, curlews, hares and foxes. Sometimes I will sit up there for 20 minutes or so, watching the wildlife go by; one day, I hope I shall have the leisure to while away whole days drawing or painting and watching. The atmosphere and feeling of nature around me is a major influence on my work. This may seem strange when you look at some of the exotic designs in this book, but my close-to-nature existence instils the desire to stitch all varieties of fauna and flora.

All the designs in this book are drawn from creatures and scenes that I love. I have enjoyed designing and stitching them and I hope that you derive an equal amount of

pleasure from making them too. Many of the designs are readily adaptable. For example, you could make a chair seat from a cushion design and vice versa; the Techniques section (see pages 137-41) gives details on how to convert charts. In addition, any of the designs could be framed with fabric so that they become larger cushions, or extended lengthways with complementary fabric to make pillows. You could also frame and hang many of the designs as pictures, rather than making them into cushions or chair seats. Stitchers often ask what else they can make besides cushions, but at the same time people usually want to make pieces that are useful. I have tried to make all the designs appealing in their own right so that they do not necessarily have to be useful!

Although all the designs in this book are charted, I hope that, for some of you, they will act as a starting point for your own creative flow. Feel free to change elements if you wish and in general use the designs as a source for your own inspiration.

# FLAMBOYANT
# FLOWERS

*The beauty, colours and variety of flowers have been a constant source of inspiration. There is a special interest in transforming a rose from one design sphere to another, for example from a china plate to a woollen hanging, that never ceases to fascinate.*

When I first started to paint and design, flowers were the subjects that particularly attracted me. At that time, I was living in a workshop community, one of whose founder members was Lillian Delevoryas – the other was Kaffe Fassett – and she happened to be painting flowers more than any other subjects. The garden was in full bloom so flowers were the obvious choice of subject when I started to paint too.

*RIGHT: An abundance of rhododendrons frames the beautiful*
*lake and bridge at Stourhead in Wiltshire, the view used in the Pink Roses*
*Cushion on page 14 (The Garden Picture Library / Nigel Francis).*

Flowers have always been important to me. When we lived in Somerset, I loved seeing the moors purple with heather combined with golden gorse, which seemed to flower in profusion all the time; and North Hill, above Minehead, was a blaze of bright magenta rhododendrons. The woods used to be full of primroses and bluebells and, later on, honeysuckle and willowherb. As I spent nearly all my time either walking or riding, I was constantly seeing all these flowers and their glorious colours.

It was not until I met Kaffe Fassett and Lillian Delevoryas, however, that there seemed any likelihood that I would try to paint or record in some way the flowers and surroundings that inspired me, and it was due to their encouragement that I finally did. It was Kaffe who led me to the Victoria and Albert Museum in London and showed me the diversity to which flowers have been used as a design element and to what effect. Working with Kaffe, and looking at all the material he drew from as inspiration for his designs, showed me how one can use themes from china, paintings, textiles, wood, and even peeling doors, and make them your own. There is a special interest to be had from transforming a rose or a butterfly from one design sphere to another, for example, from a china plate to a woollen hanging which never ceases to fascinate.

No matter how often flowers have been used as decoration, there seems to be no difficulty in finding a new way of portraying them. I have always enjoyed the fact that you can sit down to paint a vase of flowers with another person and then discover that the painted results are never the same, even when you both paint the flowers in a figurative way; it seems that no two people see things in exactly the same manner.

It would have been easy to have filled this whole book with tapestries of flowers and gardens, but I had to restrain myself to only three designs devoted entirely to flowers. Having said that, I have managed to include flowers in most of the other designs.

This chapter features a poppy screen which could furnish a living room or bedroom, and a pair of complementary rose-bordered box cushions which would sit prettily on an ornate garden seat or perhaps in a conservatory. I envisaged them as box cushions so that the edges of the borders would not be lost, but they could be made up as ordinary cushions if preferred.

# PINK ROSES CUSHION

The Pink Roses Cushion is a mass of flamboyant roses framing a view of the park at one of my favourite gardens, Stourhead, at Stourton in Wiltshire. The present house was built by Henry Hoare, and his son, also Henry Hoare (1705-1785), created the breathtaking gardens. He made the large lake and the smaller connecting ones by simply damming the River Stour. He also planted contrasting native trees, mainly spruce, oak and beech 'in large masses as the shades are in painting, to contrast the dark masses with the light ones'. I find it incredible that one can plant trees to create the effect of a painting, especially when you consider the length of time trees take to mature.

Henry Hoare was like most English gentlemen of his time, being extremely knowledgeable as far as the classics were concerned; this is reflected in his garden vision. He set out to create Arcadian groves and pastoral vistas, with the appropriate buildings set therein – the Temple of Flora, the Panthéon, the Temple of Apollo, and the Grotto with a beckoning statue of Neptune.

Stourhead was quite an accomplishment. It must be one of the most wonderful parklands to walk around in this country. At some stage I would like to design a set of small panels illustrating all of these buildings with different flowered borders.

For the roses in the design, I worked from drawings and watercolours that I had painted previously, and from some of the wonderful photographs taken by Clay Perry, who happens to be one of my favourite garden photographers.

## MATERIALS

CANVAS:

*1 piece, gauge size 10; measuring 60 x 60cm (24 x 24in), which allows a 5cm (2in) surround for stretching*

*Actual size of work: 50 x 50cm (20 x 20in)*

PATERNA YARNS:

*Off White 262 (2)*

*Daffodil 760*

*Mustard 711*

*Old Gold 752*

*Marigold 801*

*Autumn Yellow 720*

*Golden Brown 441*

*Loden Green 690 (2), 691 (4), 692 (4), 693 (3) and 694*

*Lime Green 670*

*Pine Green 660 (3) and 662*

*Teal Blue 521*

*Seafarer D501*

*Pearl Grey 213*

*Cobalt Blue 544 and 545*

*Ice Blue 552*

*Periwinkle 343*

*Dusty Pink 915 (5)*

*American Beauty 900 (2), 904 (3) and 905 (5)*

*Hot Pink 961 and 962 (2)*

*Cranberry 940 (3) and 942 (5)*

*Fuchsia 353*

Stitch the cushion in random long stitch, using two strands of yarn throughout *(see page 138)*. When the stitching is completed, stretch the piece and make the canvas up into a box cushion, following the instructions on page 140. Alternatively, if you prefer, you can make the canvas up into an ordinary cushion *(see page 139)*.

18

20

# YELLOW ROSES CUSHION

The yellow roses surrounding this view create an entirely different feeling of stillness and mystery, combined with the more enclosed garden. The scene is from the garden at Knightshayes in Devon. I have a great fondness for huge sculpted yews which contrast here with mature trees, and enclose a tranquil lily pond. This used to be a Victorian bowling green and most of the

garden was laid out with that era's formality, but from the 1940s onwards it has been 'deformalized' and much has been given over to grassy walks and topiary.

One of the most wonderful features is the Garden in the Wood – the name itself is lovely while how it came about is even more delightful. Each year, from the late 1950s right up to the early 1970s, the owners of Knightshayes, Sir John and Lady Amory, reclaimed a part of the wood. This reclaimed area – about the size of a tennis court – was brought back into the garden by thinning the trees and planting among them peonies, magnolias, azaleas, rhododendrons and a mass of other flowering shrubs and bulbs. Climbing roses were also encouraged to wrap themselves around the branches of the trees. The Garden in the Wood now covers about 30 acres of enchantment.

In my design, the yellow roses are taken from my drawings and sketches, as well as from photographs.

*LEFT: The lily pond at Knightshayes in Devon, surrounded by sculpted yew hedges (National Trust Photographic Library / Stephen Robson). RIGHT: The same view stitched and framed with a border of needlepoint roses.*

## MATERIALS

CANVAS:

*1 piece, gauge size 10; measuring 60 x 60cm (24 x 24in), which allows a 5cm (2in) surround for stretching*
*Actual size of work: 50 x 50cm (20 x 20in)*

PATERNA YARNS:

*White 261 (3)*

*Marigold 805 (2) and 803 (2)*

*Ginger 886 (2) and 883 (3)*

*Strawberry 955 and 954*

*Antique Rose D234*

*Daffodil 763 (4)*

*Autumn Yellow 727 (4), 725 (4), 723 (2) and 722*

*Copper 861 and 860*

*Ice Blue 556 and 553*

*Federal Blue 505*

*Teal Blue 523, 522 and 521*

*Pine Green 662 and 660 (4)*

*Seafarer D501*

*Loden Green 694, 693 (2), 692 (4), 691 (3) and 690 (2)*

*Lime Green 670*

Stitch the cushion in random long stitch, using two strands of yarn throughout *(see page 138)*. When the stitching is completed, stretch the piece and make the canvas up into a box cushion, following the instructions on page 140. Alternatively, you can make it up as an ordinary cushion if you prefer *(see page 139)*.

*YELLOW ROSES*
*CUSHION KEY*

| | |
|---|---|
| • | 261 |
| C | 805 |
| 3 | 886 |
| – | 955 |
| U | 954 |
| Y | D234 |
| / | 763 |
| □ | 727 |
| I | 725 |
| ↓ | 803 |
| V | 723 |
| L | 722 |
| E | 883 |
| X | 861 |
| W | 860 |
| → | 556 |
| S | 505 |
| // | 553 |
| \ | 523 |
| 6 | 522 |
| 7 | 662 |
| P | D501 |
| T | 521 |
| + | 694 |
| Z | 693 |
| △ | 670 |
| 0 | 692 |
| ∧ | 691 |
| ● | 690 |
| ⋊ | 660 |

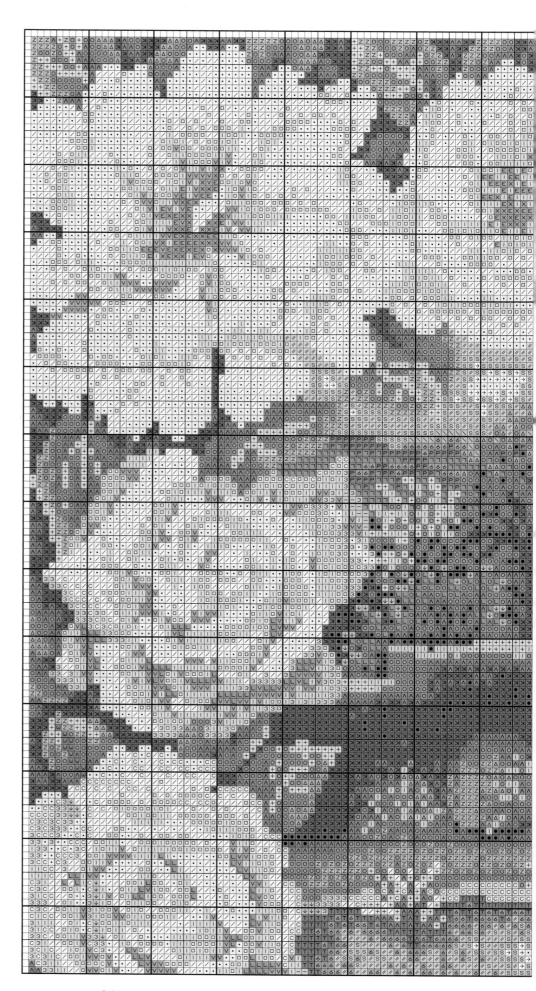

26

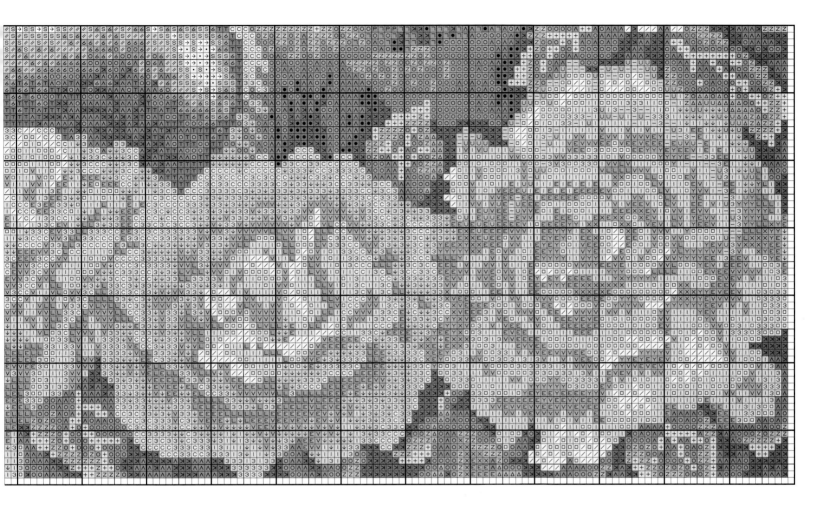

# POPPY SCREEN

I enjoyed designing and stitching the hollyhock screen for *The Tapestry Book* so much that it seemed natural to want to do another one. The choice of possible subjects to stitch was immense. My first thought was to create an underwater panorama, like a garden under the sea, full of strange corals, anemones, amazing fish and stones in a swirling aquamarine sea, but flowers came to the fore once again and the poppy idea took over. I might stitch an underwater panorama next time!

My first inspiration for stitching poppies came from Georgia O'Keefe's voluptuous paintings of huge oriental poppies in wonderful close-up views. I have always loved her work. In her writings, she has said that no one else sees the flowers she paints as she does, and although that is true, I feel very close to seeing them with her eyes because I can see all the different shades of scarlet, orange, gold and pink that she paints.

Oriental poppies are so extraordinary both in their size and texture that they almost appear unreal, especially when they first unfold from their buds. At that point they look as if they are made from thick, heavily creased paper, but from this they become gloriously inspiring, floating flowers.

Although the poppies in the fields around where I live are not the oriental variety that I have stitched in the screen, they give the same impression of vivid colour. For the fields and hills portrayed here, I took photographs and made sketches of the countryside around my home in Stafford-shire, looking towards the Manifold Valley, and worked from these. It was a great pleasure to have an excuse for wandering around the hills and spending lots of time outside because the stitching part is not so easy to work on outdoors, at least until all the colours are decided upon.

It is quite a challenge designing and stitching something as large as the screen, using a limited number of colours and making it look true to life, but it is one that I always enjoy.

*LEFT: The bold colours and contrasting textures of oriental poppies lift the spirits and are truly inspiring (Michelle Garrett).*

## MATERIALS

CANVAS:

*3 pieces, gauge size 7.6; measuring 155 x 45cm
(62 x 18in), which allows for a 5cm (2in) surround
for stretching*

*Actual size of each panel: 145 x 45cm (58 x 18in)*

PATERNA YARNS:

*Charcoal 221 (2)*

*American Beauty 901 (5)*

*Strawberry 950 (8) and 953 (2)*

*Christmas Red 970 (7)*

*Rusty Rose 931*

*Salmon 842 (8), 843 (3), 844 (3) and 845 (3)*

*Bittersweet 833 (3)*

*Rust 875*

*Blue Spruce 531 (9)*

*Forest Green 600 (7)*

*Loden Green 691 (4), 692 (9), 693 (9), 694 (8)
and 695 (5)*

*Daffodil 762*

*Mustard 712*

*White 260 (3)*

*Cool Grey 236 (2)*

*Warm Grey 256 (3)*

*Periwinkle 344*

*Pearl Grey 210*

*Cobalt Blue 544 and 545 (2)*

SCREEN:

*See Suppliers on page 143*

As this screen is such a large project, only one of the panels is charted, but if you work a mirror image of the chart for the central panel, this will produce a very similar effect to the screen I have stitched. Copy the chart exactly for panels 1 and 3, then for panel 2 either work the chart from right to left, or copy panel 1 from right to left if you find that easier.

If you would prefer to use a more artistic approach and give yourself more freedom, you could cut out a piece of cartridge paper to scale (145 x 45cm/58 x 18in) and mark on it roughly with pencil where you want the poppies to be, ensuring that they finish at approximately the same height as they do on the original panel. When you are happy with these, make strong enough ink markings for you to be able to see and trace them through when you have your canvas over them. Then place the canvas, with the outer borders marked with permanent pen, on top of the cartridge paper and copy the rough outlines of the flowers on to the canvas. Use the chart to choose and stitch the poppies as you wish,

and fill in with foliage by using sections of the chart up to the edges of your flowers. It sounds complicated but it is not in practice, and with a little bit of confidence and some thought as to where to position your flowers, you will end up with a beautiful screen that you have partly designed yourself.

Stitch the design in random long stitch, using three threads of yarn throughout *(see page 138)*. Stretch each finished panel, mount each in turn around the filler, and fasten them into the screen frame *(see p141)*.

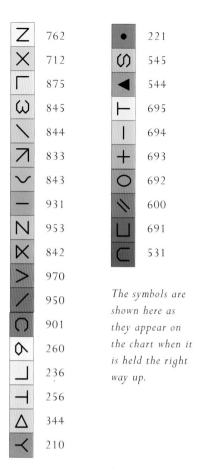

| | |
|---|---|
| 762 | |
| 712 | |
| 875 | |
| 845 | |
| 844 | |
| 833 | |
| 843 | |
| 931 | |
| 953 | |
| 842 | |
| 970 | |
| 950 | |
| 901 | |
| 260 | |
| 236 | |
| 256 | |
| 344 | |
| 210 | |

| | |
|---|---|
| 221 | |
| 545 | |
| 544 | |
| 695 | |
| 694 | |
| 693 | |
| 692 | |
| 600 | |
| 691 | |
| 531 | |

*The symbols are shown here as they appear on the chart when it is held the right way up.*

The Poppy Screen chart is on pages 36-39 and is laid out in the following way:

Part 1 on page 36

Part 2 on page 37

Part 3 on page 38

Part 4 on page 39

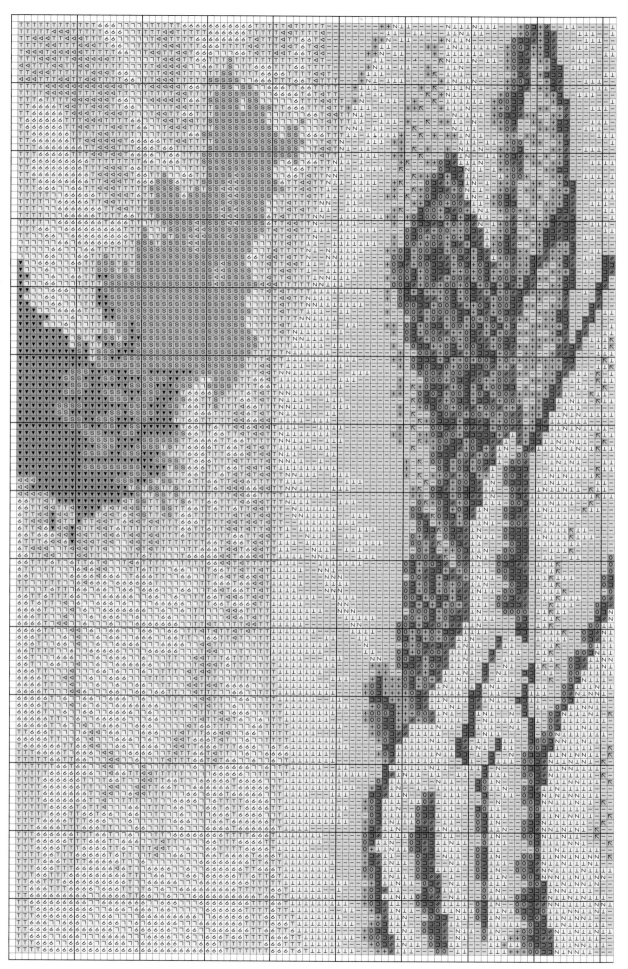

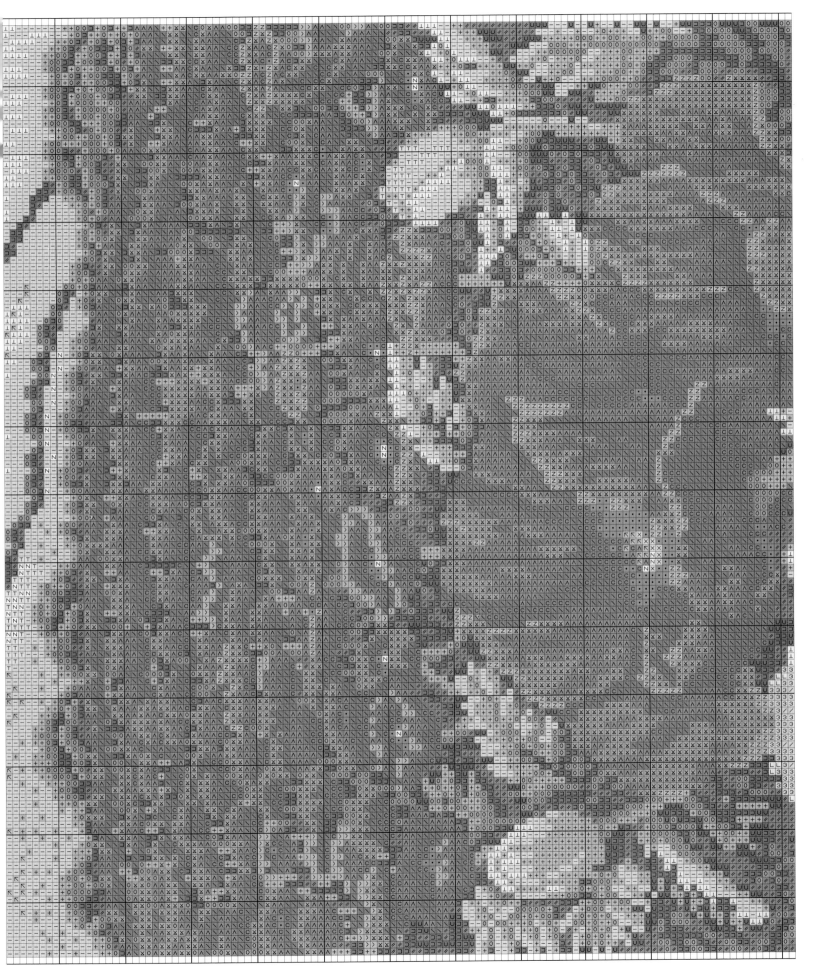

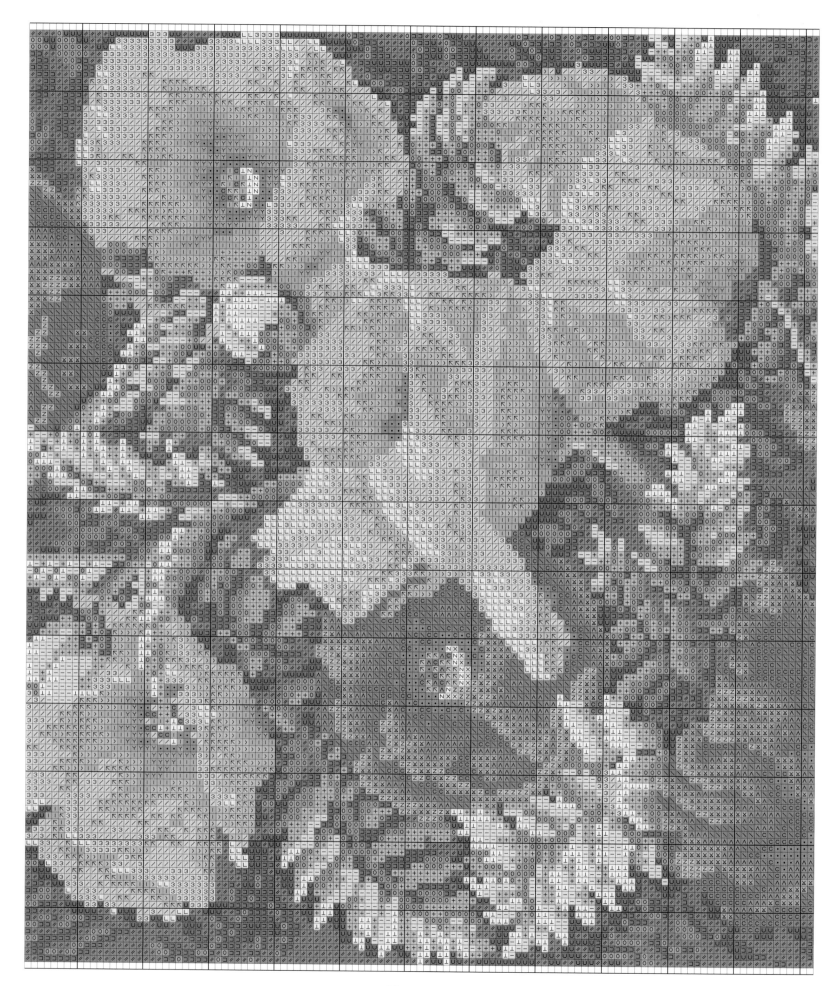

# PATTERNS IN NATURE

*Flying birds have a distinctive
rhythmical movement which can be used to create
wonderful patterns and images in tapestry.*

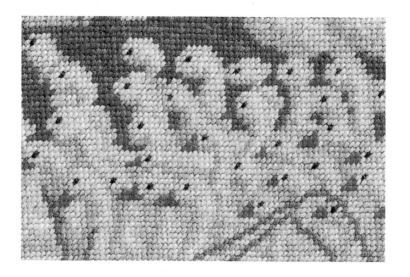

I love the patterns of birds flying, whether it is the ragged dance of crows who always seem to come out to play in great numbers when there's a high wind blowing, or the moving pattern of geese flying overhead. I often see three grey herons flying over my house, trying to decide on the best bit of stream to land by; they remind me of Japanese fabrics which portray cranes flying in patterns.

Patterns and images form the work base for the artist and designer. Some people seem to be drawn to logical repeated patterns while others, including myself, lean more towards random formations which nevertheless follow a flow and rhythm all their own. Although birds are the source for these designs, I was equally inspired by groups of zebras, butterflies, deer, seals, penguins, trees and all manner of other creatures.

*RIGHT: The dense
flurry of pastel-
coloured snow geese
taking off inspired
the Snow Geese
Firescreen on page 42
(Super Stock Ltd/John
Warden).*

40

# SNOW GEESE FIRESCREEN

While looking through magazines and cuttings one day, I came across a stupendous photograph of snow geese taking off (*see page 41*). There was such a flurry of activity in the picture. The geese in the foreground looked so amusing; they were all lined up, all facing the same way as if waiting for take-off runway clearance from some invisible air traffic controller. In fact, there were probably thousands of geese in the photograph, almost as far as the eye could see, so I concentrated on just a small section for this firescreen design, which seemed to fulfill the dictionary definition of the word pattern as 'a random combination of shapes and colours' (*The Oxford Complete Wordfinder*).

When researching for more photographic references of snow geese, I found that in one phase of their growth, the adults have a sizeable area of feathers which are lavender-blue in colour, and these geese are known as Blue Geese. I had already seen shades of lavender, mauve and blue in the initial photograph, so this information satisfied my own findings.

I enjoyed working with muted colours as a change from the more brilliant colours I usually use. The pale pearly shadows give an impression of brightness which you might not expect from such pale shades. It was fun stitching the geese, making each one different from its companions. The completed needlepoint is full of life and really conveys the movements of taking off and flying.

# MATERIALS

### CANVAS:

*1 piece, gauge size 10; measuring 62.5 x 52.5cm (25 x 21in), which allows a 5cm (2in) surround for stretching*

*Actual size of work: 52.5 x 42.5cm (21 x 17in)*

### PATERNA YARNS:

| | |
|---|---|
| *White 260 (7)* | *Copper 864* |
| *Off White 261 (6)* | *Salmon 842 (2)* |
| *Plum 325 (5)* | *Periwinkle 341 (2), 342, 343 (6)* |
| *Warm Grey 256 (5)* | *and 344 (3)* |
| *Pearl Grey 212, 211 and 210* | *Strawberry 950* |
| *Charcoal 221 (2)* | *Grape 314 (2)* |

### FIRESCREEN:

*See page 143 for suppliers*

Work this design in tent stitch, which is more traditional for a firescreen, using two threads of yarn throughout *(see page 138)*. When the stitching is finished, stretch the canvas and make it up into a firescreen *(see page 141)*.

*SNOW GEESE*
*FIRESCREEN KEY*

| Symbol | Number |
|---|---|
| ● | 260 |
| P | 261 |
| — | 325 |
| 3 | 864 |
| ∧ | 842 |
| U | 950 |
| / | 314 |
| S | 344 |
| ◊ | 343 |
| X | 342 |
| I | 341 |
| ◁ | 256 |
| ˩ | 212 |
| \\ | 211 |
| Y | 210 |
| ● | 221 |

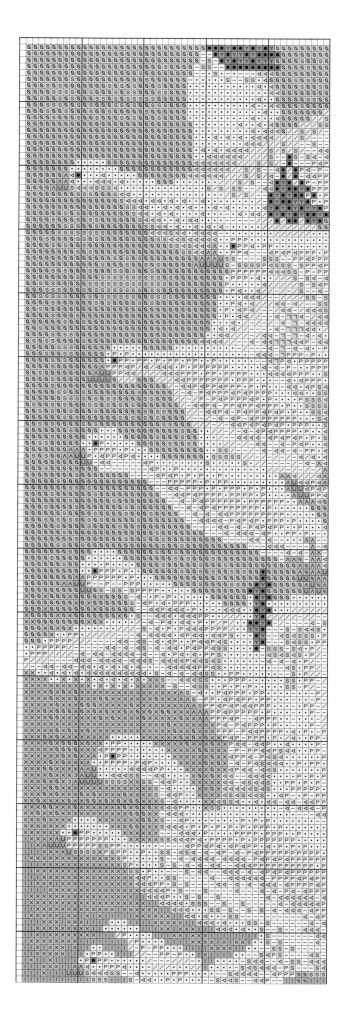

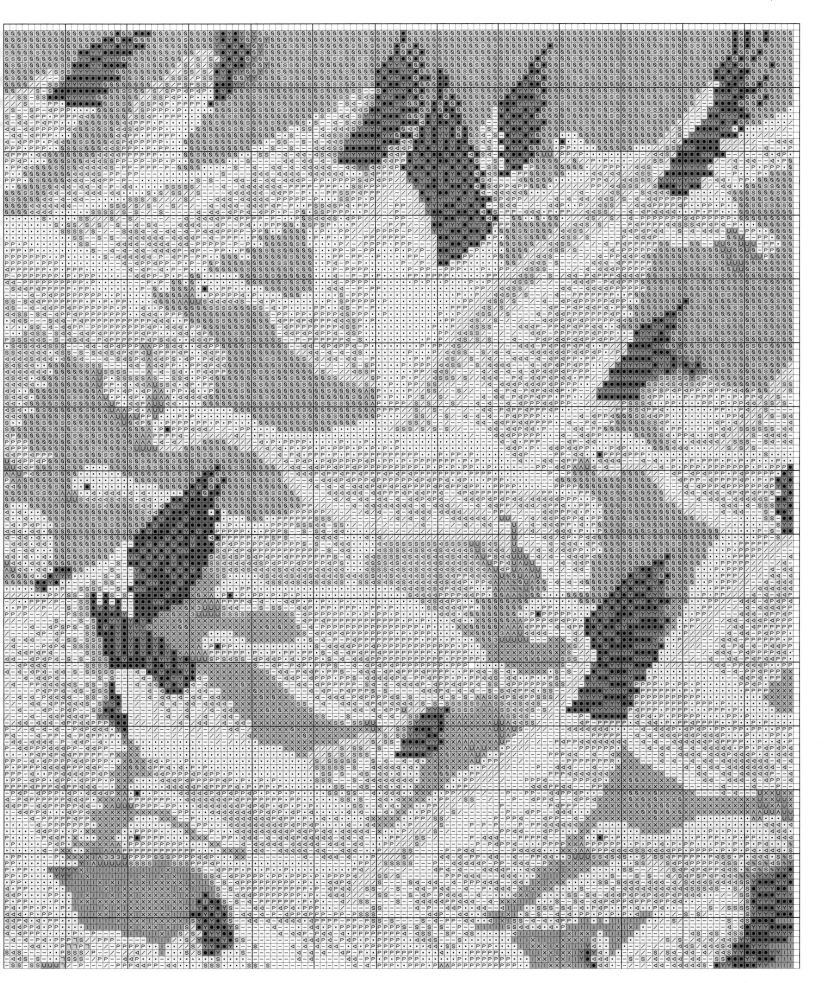

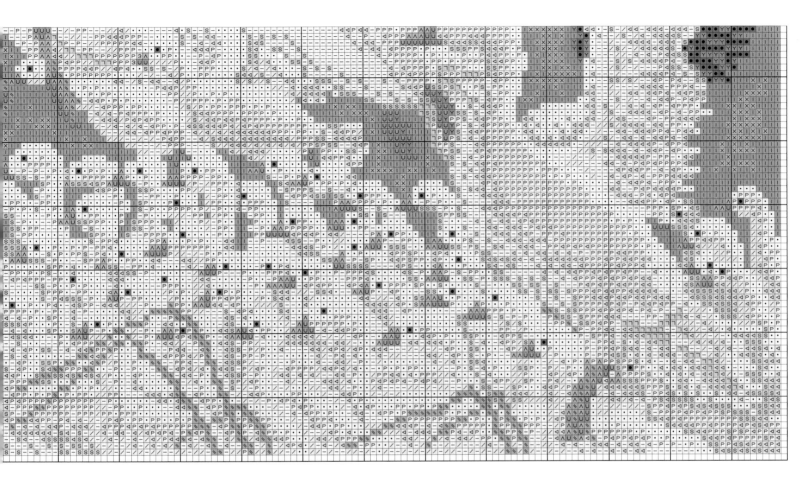

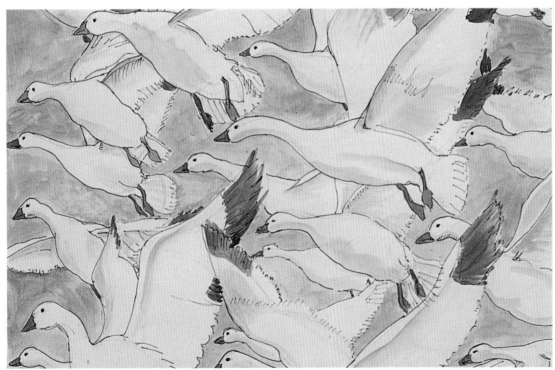

# HUMMINGBIRDS CHAIR SEAT

This chair seat was a lovely piece to design and stitch, and the iridescent colours were a delight to work with. I enjoyed poring over photographs of these exquisite, minuscule birds, and I also had fun finding out more about them. I always seem to get sidetracked into reading any text when looking for photographs, but I did extend my knowledge by doing so! I discovered, for instance, that there are around 300 species of hummingbird living in the Americas and one species migrates as far north as Alaska. Somehow, I cannot picture a hummingbird in Alaska; I had always assumed that they stayed in tropical areas. However, having worked this design, I am now determined to create a series of different coloured hummingbirds and flowers in brilliant colours to light up the rooms in my house during our cold, dark and often sunless days of winter.

*Hovering iridescent hummingbirds and hibiscus inspired this mirror-image tapestry design, worked on different coloured backgrounds for this cushion and the chairseat opposite.*

## MATERIALS

CANVAS:

*1 piece, gauge size 10; measuring*

*52.5 x 50cm (21 x 20in),*

*which allows for a 5cm (2in)*

*surround for stretching*

*Actual size of work:*

*42.5 x 35 x 40cm*

*(17 x 14 x 16in)*

PATERNA YARNS:

*Mustard 711*

*Marigold 801*

*Plum 326*

*Dusty Pink 914*

*Cranberry 944*

*American Beauty 904, 902*

  *and 900*

*Strawberry 952 and 950*

*Charcoal 221*

*Loden Green 694, 693 and 692*

*Christmas Green 696*

*Hunter Green 610*

*Cobalt Blue 542*

*Sky Blue 580*

*Caribbean Blue 592 (3) and*

  *593 (4)*

This design is stitched in tent stitch and the right half of the design mirrors the left half exactly. I have even stitched it so that the stitches are mirrored from the centre line. This means that the left half is stitched in the usual way from right to left, while the right half is stitched from left to right. However, it is not essential to mirror your stitches like this – the stitches can go in the usual way if you prefer, as in the cushion version of this design *(see page 52)*.

The chart illustrates one half of the design and there are two easy ways of following it. First, mark the centre of the canvas. Then you can either work the whole of the chart as shown, then copy your own stitching by working backwards on the other half. Alternatively, you can follow the chart from the centre line back out to the outer edge.

The chart is squared-off as for a cushion. If you would like to adapt it for a chair seat, see page 140.

Stitch the chair seat in tent stitch, using two threads of yarn throughout *(see page 138)*. When the stitching is finished, stretch and mount the canvas on to your particular chair *(see page 140)*.

| | | |
|---|---|---|
| *HUMMINGBIRDS* | O | 711 |
| *CHAIR SEAT KEY* | X | 801 |
| | T | 326 |
| | Z | 914 |
| | N | 944 |
| | 3 | 904 |
| | V | 952 |
| | △ | 950 |
| | ⌀ | 902 |
| | ⌐ | 900 |
| | ＼ | 221 |
| | • | 694 |
| | ← | 693 |
| | L | 692 |
| | + | 696 |
| | C | 610 |
| | / | 542 |
| | – | 580 |
| | □ | 593 |
| | I | 592 |

To stitch this design as a cushion, use a piece of canvas measuring 50 x 50cm (20 x 20in) and work the stitching to a 40cm (16in) square. It is interesting to see the effect of stitching a different background colour for the cushion, and I have used a vivid yellow (Paterna shade: Lime Green 672) instead of the two shades of Caribbean Blue (592 and 593) shown on the chair seat key, which gives an excitingly different and vibrant result. For instructions on making up a cushion, see page 139.

*ABOVE: I drew upon the colouring and flight of this broadbill hummingbird for my design, but changed the flower to hibiscus (Super Stock Ltd).*

# EXOTIC FLOWERS AND FOLIAGE

*The rainforest has always seemed to me to epitomize
the exotic. Full of gorgeously coloured plants
and creatures, there is enough inspiration to create
an entire book of needlepoint designs.*

Strange, brightly coloured plants and creatures
are to be found everywhere in the rainforest, from the Amazon lily *(Nymphaea amazonica
victoria)*, the brilliant flamingo flower *(Anthurium* sp*)* and the scarlet passionflower
*(Passiflora coccinea)*, to the exquisite tiny tree frogs, which can be found in miniature ponds
forming in the flame-coloured bromeliads.

It would be a treat to create a whole book of designs devoted entirely to the exotica of
the rainforest. Who knows, perhaps one day, I shall go on field trips and obtain first-hand
sketches and watercolours of my subjects. Until then, however, I shall have to rely on the
Palm House in Kew Gardens, London, for examples of exotic plants and for the
experience of humidity and density!

*RIGHT: A beautiful
diminutive squirrel tree
frog pauses in the
scarlet petals of a
hibiscus — a wonderful
subject for a needlepoint
(Image Bank / James
Carmichael).*

# JUNGLE WATERFALL HANGING

In this piece I wanted to stitch as many beautiful plants, creatures and elements as I could without overcrowding the design; my aim was to create a hanging that would be a pleasure to look at over and over again. My own preference for hangings and paintings that you want to be able to live with for some considerable time, is that they should hold an element of mystery so that you are not able to see everything there is to see immediately. This does not necessarily mean incorporating hidden objects in the design; the mystery can be in the effect of shadows and the depths they create. In this hanging, the little snake wrapped around the heliconia *(top right)*, is probably not immediately apparent. This was taken from a flower reference I was using which just happened to have a newly hatched boa coiled around it!

The monkeys shown here are the exquisite, diminutive squirrel monkeys, who have the most beautiful little faces and tufted elfin ears. As soon as I had seen and

drawn these monkeys, I knew I would like to produce other needlepoints with monkeys as the main subject. Another lovely idea would be to make some cushions or runners which match elements of the jungle waterfall hanging. There could be a parrot design showing the scarlet macaw in more detail, a monkey design and a design of the boa coiled around the glorious flame-like heliconia. However, there is only so much space in a book and, for the time being, these two projects will have to suffice in reflecting my desire to make tapestries of these particular climes and habitats.

## MATERIALS

CANVAS:

*1 piece, gauge size 10; measuring
75 x 75cm (30 x 30in), which
allows a 5cm (2in) surround for
stretching*

*Actual size of work: 75 x 75cm
(30 x 30in)*

PATERNA YARNS:

*White 260 (3)*

*Off White 262 (4)*

*American Beauty 900 (2) and
    902 (3)*

*Dusty Pink 913 (3)*

*Fuchsia 353*

*Christmas Red 970 (3)*

*Spice 851 (2) and 853 (2)*

*Mustard 712 (2)*

*Sunny Yellow 771 (2) and 773 (2)*

*Golden Brown 440*

*Old Gold 751*

*Autumn Yellow 725*

*Olive Green 652*

*Hunter Green 610 (6) and
    612 (3)*

*Loden Green 690 (4), 691 (13),
    692 (13), 693 (10) and
    694 (6)*

*Pine Green 660 (12) and 665 (4)*

*Seafarer D503 (3)*

*Caribbean Blue 593 (2)*

*ABOVE: A waterfall splashes among
giant tropical ferns and foliage
(Zefa Pictures / John Carnemolla).*

This wall hanging was stitched in random
long stitch using two threads of yarn
throughout, so that although it is large, it
was stitched quite quickly *(see page 138)*. The
hanging could be stitched in tent stitch if
you prefer, but it will take much longer to
complete and will have a different look and
feel to it. Once stitched, the canvas needs to
be stretched and made up *(see page 139)*. It
can either be framed and hung as a picture,
or backed and used as a wall hanging. Wall
hangings can look sumptuous if they are
framed in a complementary fabric.

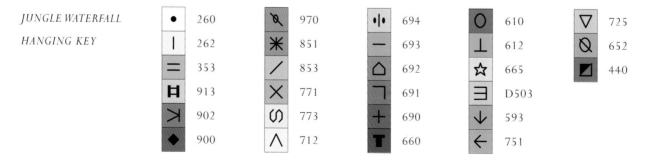

# ORCHIDS CUSHION

Having been fascinated for a long time by begonias and orchids – I have used both for still life paintings and for subjects of needlepoint designs – it was a revelation to find that these grow quite naturally in chaotic profusion in tropical rainforests. The idea of designing an orchids cushion has been in my mind ever since I

painted a watercolour of grapes and orchids some years ago. But, after some trial sketches, this design turned out to be orchids and begonia leaves – the grapes seemed more of an English greenhouse idea than a hothouse jungle one.

I gave myself the go-ahead to use artistic licence and have depicted types of orchid that may well not grow in the same area as begonias, but they look very good together. The orchids stitched here are a yellowish-green *Cymbidium* and a magenta *Dendrobium*. There are more than 1,400 species of *Dendrobium* and it is one of the most diversified of the orchid family. The *Cymbidium* is widely grown because of its ease of cultivation and its exceptionally long-lasting flowers. There are 70 species of *Cymbidium*, from which thousands of hybrids have been cultivated; they come in the most wonderful colours with masses of flowers on each stem.

You can never tell exactly how a design is going to work until it is completely stitched, and when this was finished I really liked the effect of the bold orchid leaves placed against the more complex begonia leaves. I think it creates a wealth of interest and subtlety of tone in what is quite a dramatic design.

The next time I use this idea, I intend to leave more room for the begonia leaves as they are so beautiful. I have had a long-term love affair with begonias and at one time I possessed about 20, mostly grown from leaves taken from other people's plants – usually with their permission. One of the things that really fascinates me is that no two plants in my experience have ever had exactly the same leaves. I expect it is the same with every living thing, whether creature, plant or human being – every single one is unique.

You could make this cushion design up into a chair seat if you prefer; simply alter the dimensions to suit your chair (*for instructions, see page 138*).

### MATERIALS

CANVAS:

*1 piece, gauge size 10; measuring 50 x 50cm*
*(20 x 20in), which allows for a 5cm (2in) surround*
*for stretching*
*Actual size of work: 40 x 40cm (16 x 16in)*

PATERNA YARNS:

*Spring Green 634, 633 (2) and 632 (4)*
*Loden Green 694 (2), 693, 692 (2) and 691 (2)*
*Hunter Green 612 (3)*
*American Beauty 900 (2) and 902*
*Olive Green 652 (2)*
*Pine Green 660*
*Sunny Yellow 771 and 772*
*White 261 (2)*
*Spice 851*
*Fuchsia 353 (3)*
*Dusty Pink 913 (3)*

. ORCHIDS
CUSHION
KEY

| Symbol | Number |
|---|---|
| ⊥ | 913 |
| 1 | 353 |
| ● | 900 |
| ⌐ | 902 |
| ◇ | 851 |
| — | 261 |
| ∧ | 771 |
| I | 772 |
| → | 660 |
| 9 | 691 |
| = | 652 |
| ▽ | 692 |
| ∴ | 612 |
| Y | 693 |
| \ | 694 |
| ◆ | 632 |
| + | 633 |
| ❚❚ | 634 |

*This chart is shown sideways on.*

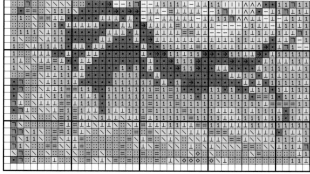

This needlepoint is worked in tent stitch *(see page 138)*, using two threads of yarn throughout. You could use random long stitch if you prefer, bearing in mind that this will result in a different texture and look, and is not suitable for a chair seat unless it is reinforced. When you have finished stitching, you will need to stretch and make up the cushion *(see page 139)*.

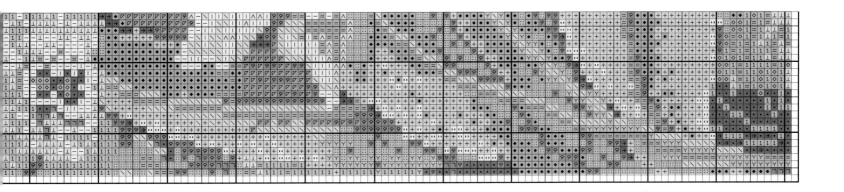

# FISH AND SHELLS

*The beauty of the sea and the variety of
the creatures that live within it are sources of
never-ending pleasure and inspiration
to me; the range of colours displayed underwater
is a kaleidoscope for tapestry designs.*

For most of my childhood I lived by the sea, and it's only in recent years that I have lived so far inland. I've always loved pottering along the seashore, looking for jellyfish, crabs, shells and fish in the rock pools along the beaches. The sea was fascinating in a different way. Although swimming in it was great fun, I didn't like not being able to see the bottom – you were never quite sure whether it was seaweed, fish or monsters that were touching you under the water!

Swimming in the sea in Israel was wonderful. Here there were great transparent depths to explore. Some time later I lived for four years in Croatia, much of which was spent swimming in the Adriatic, which made me even more unwilling to brave the cold seas off the English coast again. It's a pity that where the sea is lovely and clear around the English coastline, and there is a lot to see underwater, the water is so icy.

*RIGHT: The myriad hues
of yellow and violet
fairy basslets swimming
through the coral
would make a wonderful
needlepoint (Zefa
Pictures).*

# Hawaiian Hawkfish Cushion

My feelings for the sea are similar to those for the rainforest and the whole of nature. Its beauty and variety are sources of never-ending pleasure and inspiration to me, so I was pleased to include the creatures of the sea in this book. For these projects I chose two gloriously coloured tropical fish and teamed them up with a variety of shells to provide a colourful seascape. These designs just scratch the surface of this theme, and there are still many more seascapes waiting to be designed, when I have the time.

I absolutely fell for the Hawaiian hawkfish when I first saw him, with his glorious oranges mixed with murky greeny-brown and the most beautiful orange and pink spotted mouth. Although it is not strictly realistic, I included lots of different shells around this fish in my design. Hawaiian hawkfish actually live in shallow waters and their favourite pastime is perching on coral waiting for food to go by. Then they whip out and catch it and return to their coral perch just as quickly, where they are excellently camouflaged. The shells are from different sources, some of which I collected myself. The difficulty was trying to keep the number of colours to a reasonable level while still portraying the pearly opalescence of the shells. I like the fact that the colours in this design are subtle but not sombre.

# MATERIALS

CANVAS:

*1 piece, gauge size 10; measuring 50 x 50cm*

*(20 x 20in), which allows for a 5cm (2in) surround*

*for stretching*

*Actual size of work: 40 x 40cm (16 x 16in)*

PATERNA YARNS:

*Bittersweet 833 (2) and 832 (2)*

*Salmon 841 (2)*

*Sky Blue 584*

*Old Blue 515 (2)*

*Pine Green 660*

*Forest Green 600 (2)*

*Loden Green 691 (2)*

*Olive Green 651 (2) and 652 (3)*

*Autumn Yellow 724 (2), 723 (2) and 722 (2)*

*Old Gold 753 (3) and 755 (2)*

*Cinnamon D411 (2), D425 and D419*

*Golden Brown 440 and 441*

*Donkey Brown D115*

*Spice 855*

Stitch the canvas in tent stitch, using two threads of yarn throughout *(see page 138)*. When you have finished stitching, stretch the canvas and make it up into a cushion *(see page 139)*.

When stitching this design, it is interesting to see how different the effect is of the same colours when they are used in an altered context. The oranges and blues of the fish look pale and pearly when used with the creams of the shells yet quite dense and colourful in the fish.

*HAWAIIAN HAWKFISH*

*CUSHION KEY*

| Symbol | Colour |
|---|---|
| ● | D425 |
| ⊥ | 855 |
| Z | 833 |
| ▽ | 841 |
| / | 755 |
| C | 724 |
| I | 753 |
| + | 723 |
| V | D419 |
| D | 722 |
| L | 832 |
| ◢ | D411 |
| 6 | 441 |
| 7 | 440 |
| – | D115 |
| ↓ | 652 |
| S | 651 |
| O | 691 |
| U | 600 |
| X | 660 |
| → | 515 |
| Y | 584 |

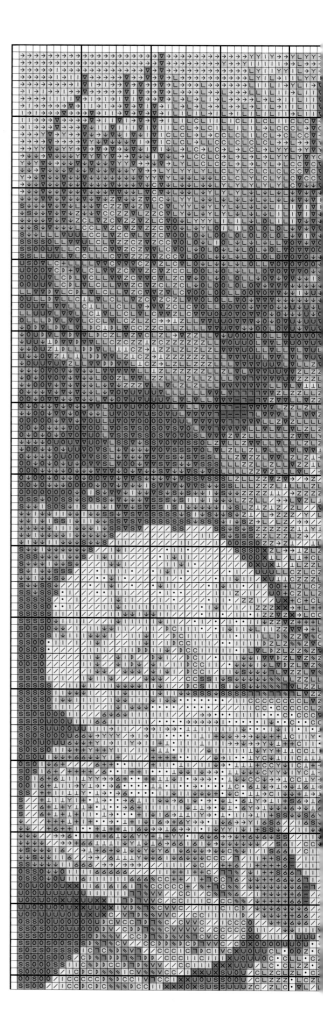

76

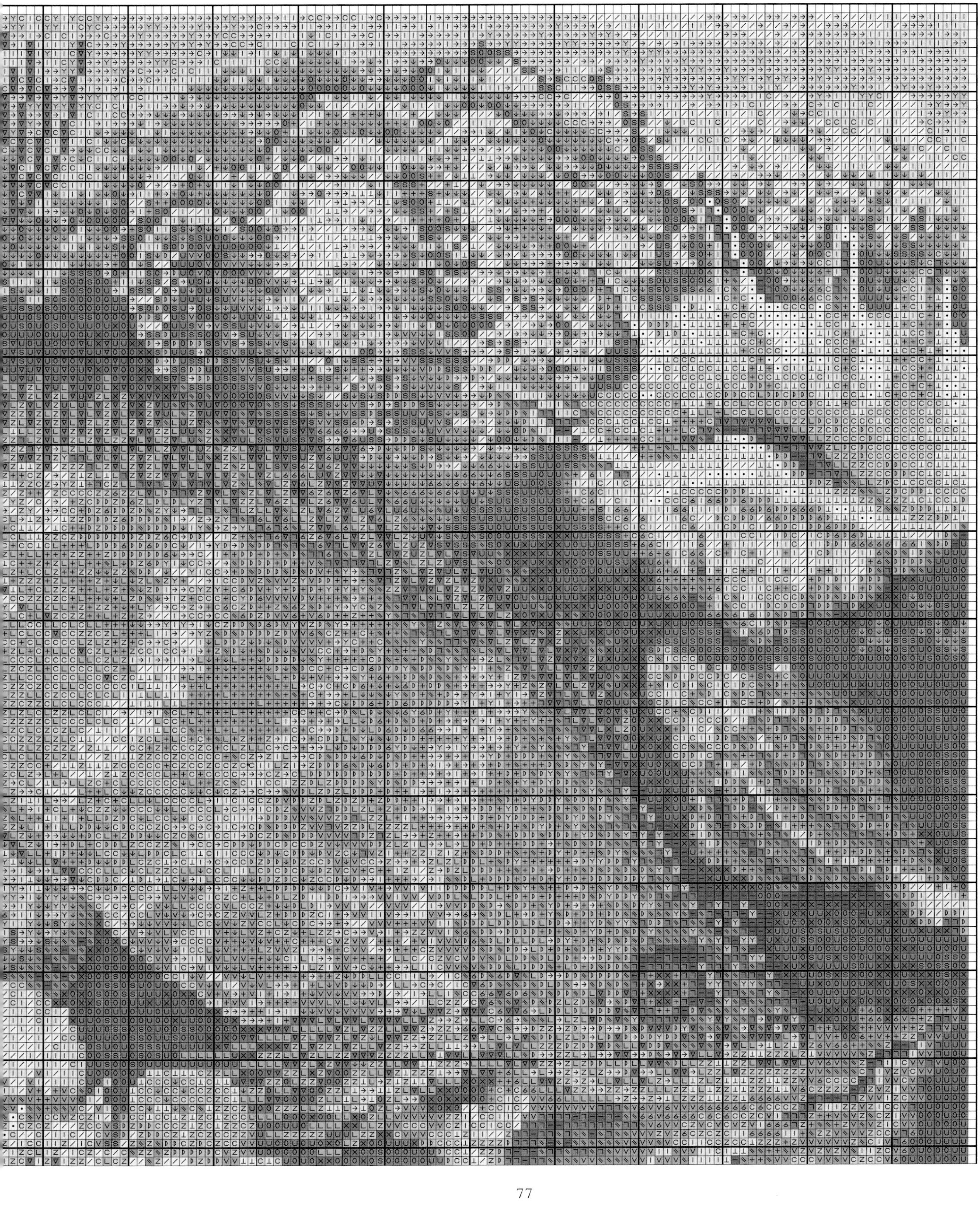

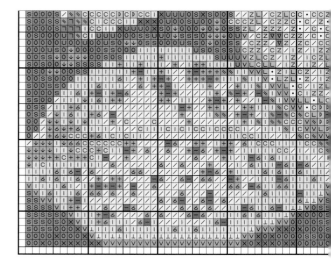

It is always fascinating stitching faces and seeing them come to life, and it is no different whether it is a person, an animal or a fish. You put in all the details that you observe and just when you think that it is remaining stubbornly unreal, it quite suddenly comes to life.

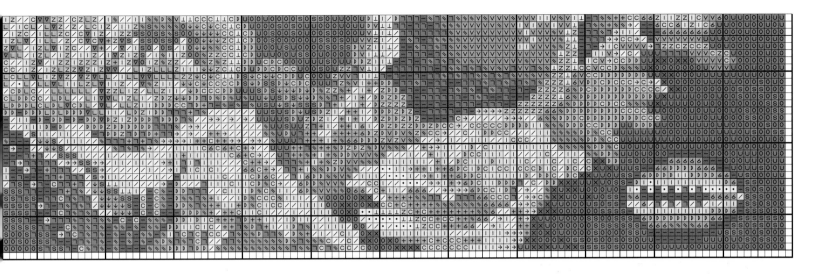

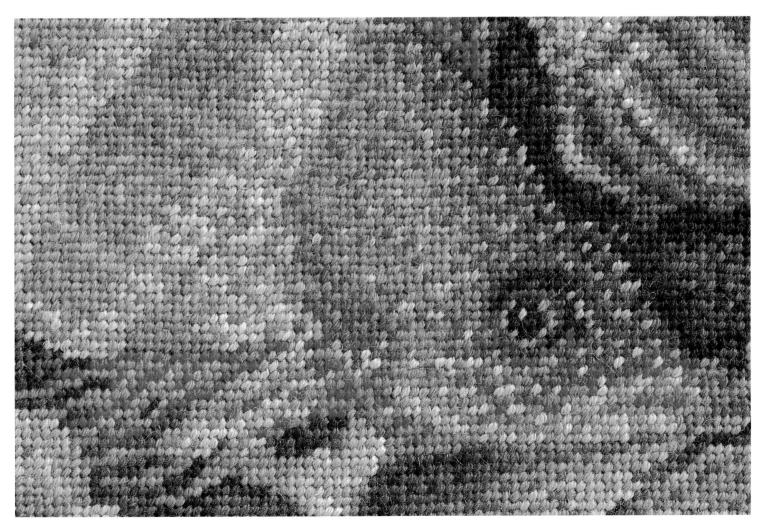

# EXQUISITE WRASSE CUSHION

I chose to feature the exquisite wrasse fish partly because of its name – it must be lovely to be described as exquisite – and partly because I wanted another coral reef fish that was completely different from the Hawaiian hawkfish. But the main reason for choosing this fish was its amazing colours. There are so many different types of tropical marine fish which would have been wonderful to stitch, that I had a difficult time choosing. However, as I had to limit the project to a sensible number of yarn colours, this helped me to decide on the actual fish.

While I was looking at tropical fish, I could not help marvelling at all the other incredible rainbow-coloured creatures living beneath the surface of the sea, such as sea slugs, anemones, shells and the coral itself. In fact, the orange plant featured above the clam in this design is the red gorgonia coral. I was also sidetracked by the text of my references and discovered a lot of interesting things about coral reef fish and their habits, and the wrasse species in

particular. I now know that wrasses of this family are hermaphrodites and start life as females; so the male exquisite wrasse I have stitched here has transformed from a female. The reason for this is that life is quite precarious for wrasse fish and this transformation gives them two chances of breeding in one lifetime. There are said to be about 400 species of wrasse and, as a group, they are extremely colourful, with great differences between adult males, females and young fish. Because of this, some species have been named twice, so the figure of 400 may be exaggerated.

The shells in the design were taken mostly from ones I have picked up here and there over the years, and some that I have shamelessly borrowed from Kaffe Fassett's *Glorious Inspiration*, but that was his intention for the book. I think these two designs work well together as cushions, as illustrated here, but they would also look wonderful as chair seats *(see page 140 on adapting a chart for a chair seat).*

## MATERIALS

CANVAS:

*1 piece, gauge size 10; measuring 50 x 50cm (20 x 20in), which allows for a 5cm (2in) surround for stretching*

*Actual size of work: 40 x 40cm (16 x 16in)*

PATERNA YARNS:

*Sky Blue 582, 583 (2) and 584 (2)*

*Tangerine 825*

*Bittersweet 835, 834 (2), 833 and 832 (2)*

*Pine Green 664, 660 and 663 (2)*

*Ocean Green D522 (2), D516*

*Loden Green 691 (2), 690 (3)*

*Olive Green 652 (2), 651 (2) and 654 (2)*

*Autumn Yellow 724 (2) and 722 (2)*

*Golden Brown 440, 441 (2) and 442*

*Teal Blue 525 (2)*

Stitch the canvas in tent stitch, using two threads of yarn throughout *(see page 138)*. When the stitching is complete, stretch the needlepoint and make it up into a cushion *(see page 139)*.

*EXQUISITE WRASSE*

*CUSHION KEY*

| Symbol | Colour |
|---|---|
| ● | 825 |
| З | 835 |
| I | 834 |
| – | 833 |
| ↓ | 832 |
| V | 654 |
| ⌐ | 442 |
| L | 724 |
| U | 722 |
| C | 441 |
| / | 440 |
| \ | 664 |
| 6 | 663 |
| N | D522 |
| ↑ | D516 |
| T | 691 |
| ◁ | 690 |
| // | 660 |
| X | 652 |
| → | 651 |
| S | 525 |
| Y | 584 |
| + | 583 |
| + | 582 |

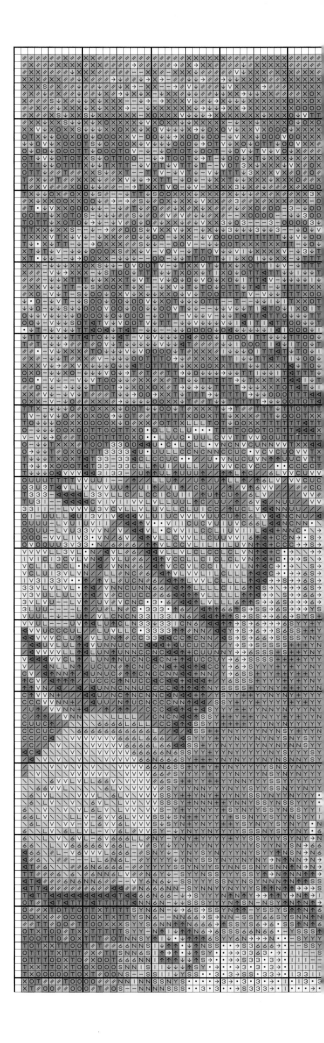

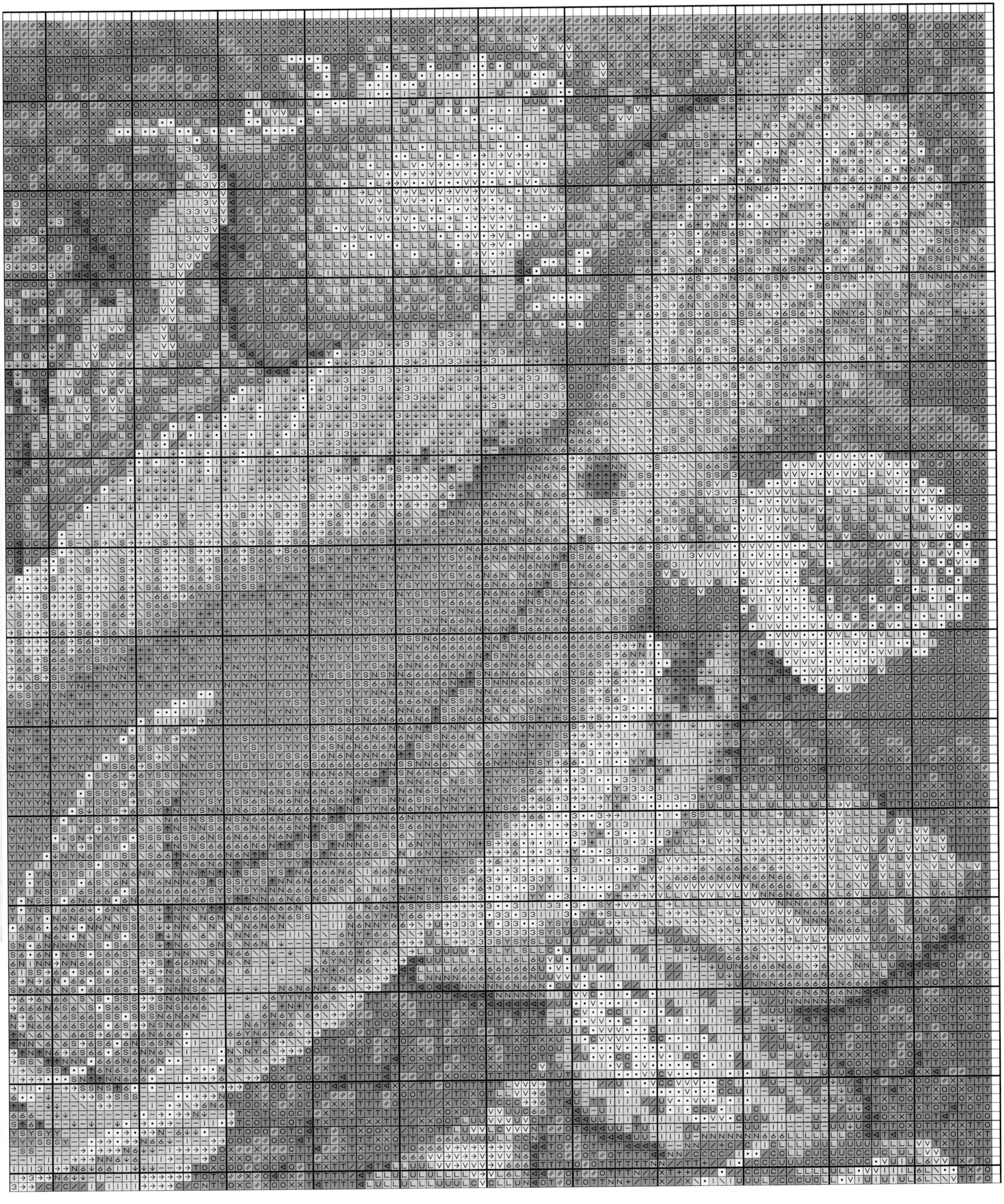

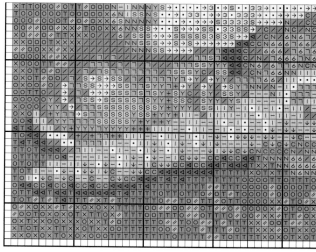

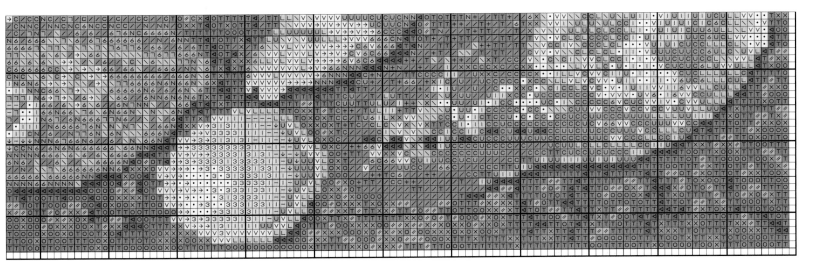

If you compare the exquisite wrasse's face with that of the Hawaiian hawkfish, you will see what different characters they are. It makes it such fun attempting to portray the character of each creature. Coral reefs are hosts to such a wide variety of sea life and they are so vividly coloured, that there seems an endless supply of inspiration.

# DESERT AND SAVANNAH

*To me, deserts are magical places; within which
brilliantly coloured cacti can flourish,
while savannah grasslands are the home to myriad
magnificent animals which make perfect
subjects for needlepoint.*

**D**eserts have long held a fascination for me,
partly because until recently they have been considered by many to be both boring and
devoid of beauty. This idea has been dispelled to a large extent by the wildlife and nature
programmes shown in recent times, and also perhaps by the magnificent scenery in the
film *Lawrence of Arabia* – I certainly thought it wonderful.

When I went to Israel in 1970, and travelled firstly through the Negev Desert and then
the Sinai Desert, my captivation was complete. I ended up living in Israel for a year. This
was before I had met Kaffe Fassett or any other like-minded people and my enthusiasm
fell mostly on deaf ears. Most of the people on the kibbutz where I was living considered

the idea of spending a week travelling around the Sinai as extremely tedious – to me it was utterly magical. It was a relief to read the following quotation and to realize that there were fellow admirers:

'… to many, visiting a desert inspires the same wonder and has the same spiritual impact as contemplating the ocean or a mountain has on others … the awesome vistas, cloudless skies, and dazzling sun afford the same sense of belonging to an ultimate reality greater than themselves as does the sight of the heavens on a starry night.' (*Wildlife of the Deserts*, by Frederic H. Wagner, Windward.)

I also like the fact that there are cold deserts too, and one of my favourite photographs is of whooper swans in a desert snowstorm looking like miniature white dunes, with their heads tucked under their wings and only the yellow flash on the sides of their beaks and eyes visible. This was one image that led to the design of the snow geese firescreen featured on page 42.

Initially, my design ideas for this chapter were of vast sandscapes and stone ruins with jewel-coloured desert wildlife, such as rainbow geckos and the colourful lubber grasshopper, in the foreground. However, although one would think that very few colours would be necessary since sand is often thought to be one colour, it actually needs an incredible array of subtly related colours to create the beauty of the desert; this, of course, was not really practical for a charted needlepoint design.

So, for the desert part of this chapter, I have contented myself with a densely packed design of cactus flowers, while for the savannah or grasslands part I chose elephants and leopards as being unusual and challenging subjects to stitch.

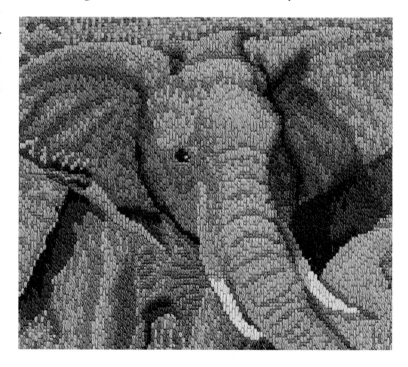

# ELEPHANTS AND LEOPARDS HANGING

Elephants are so impressive. I have always had a great fondness for them and it interested me to see whether I could make them look alive in wool – I think that they do. The bush elephant once lived throughout most of the African savannah but their range is now much reduced as people cultivate more land. I have only ever seen elephants in captivity and that is always mixed with a feeling of sadness. They are so far away from their natural habitat and they appear far too large for the English landscape; they seem aware of their own unhappiness.

In looking for ideas for the theme of savannah, I found there to be no shortage at all of design sources. The savannah is absolutely teeming with beautiful animals, birds, butterflies, grasses, trees and flowers, not to mention rivers and lakes. The idea for this particular scene was one I developed from a photograph in a book about Zimbabwe. There actually was a tree trunk growing across a clearing with two leopards resting on it; the hibiscus were also growing in a clearing, but a different one, while the elephants were featured in another photograph. I simply moved all the subjects into the one picture!

## MATERIALS

CANVAS:

*1 piece, gauge size 10; measuring 1m x 70cm*
*(40 x 28in), which allows a 5cm (2in) surround for*
*stretching*
*Actual size of work: 90 x 60cm (36 x 24in)*

PATERNA YARNS:

*Coffee Brown 421 (3)*
*Charcoal 220*
*Beige Brown 460 (3), 461 (6), 462 (9), 463 (11)*
*  and 464  (2)*
*Earth Brown 414 (4) and 413 (7)*
*Chocolate Brown 432 (3)*
*Khaki Brown 455*
*Tobacco 743 (3)*
*Autumn Yellow 722 (2) and 724 (2)*
*American Beauty 901*
*Cranberry 941*
*Strawberry 953 (2) and 955 (4)*
*Cobalt Blue 544*
*Ice Blue 553 (5) and 554 (2)*
*Old Gold 756*
*Pine Green 660 (4)*
*Hunter Green 611 (3)*
*Loden Green 691 (6), 692 (6), 693 (6) and 694 (4)*

Stitch the needlepoint in random long stitch, using two threads of yarn throughout *(see page 138)*. Although the design is quite large, it does not take forever to do because of the type of stitch. When stitching the design, bear in mind the effect that the lengths of the stitches have on the texture you are creating. You could use tent stitch if you prefer, but the texture will be different. Once the stitching is completed, the hanging needs to be stretched and finished *(see page 141)*.

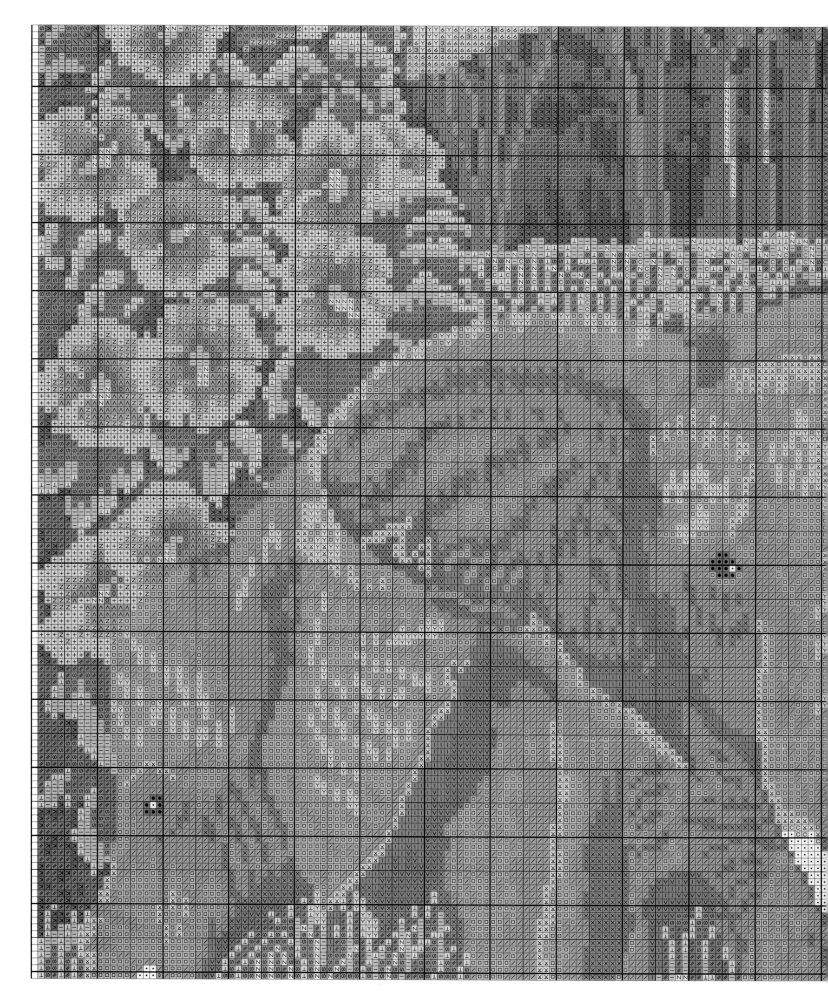

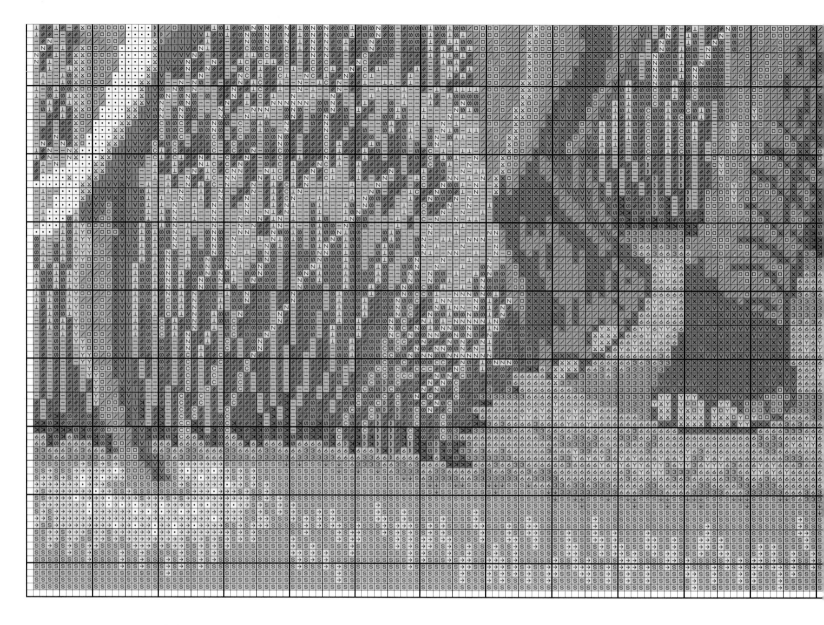

ELEPHANTS AND
LEOPARDS HANGING
KEY

| | | | | |
|---|---|---|---|---|
| • 756 | L 455 | V 460 | 0 901 | ↗ 660 |
| N 743 | X 464 | I 421 | ⊥ 694 | → 554 |
| C 724 | □ 463 | ● 220 | S 693 | S 553 |
| Y 414 | / 462 | + 955 | S 692 | ↓ 544 |
| 6 413 | X 461 | Z 953 | \ 611 | |
| D 722 | 3 432 | ∧ 941 | // 691 | |

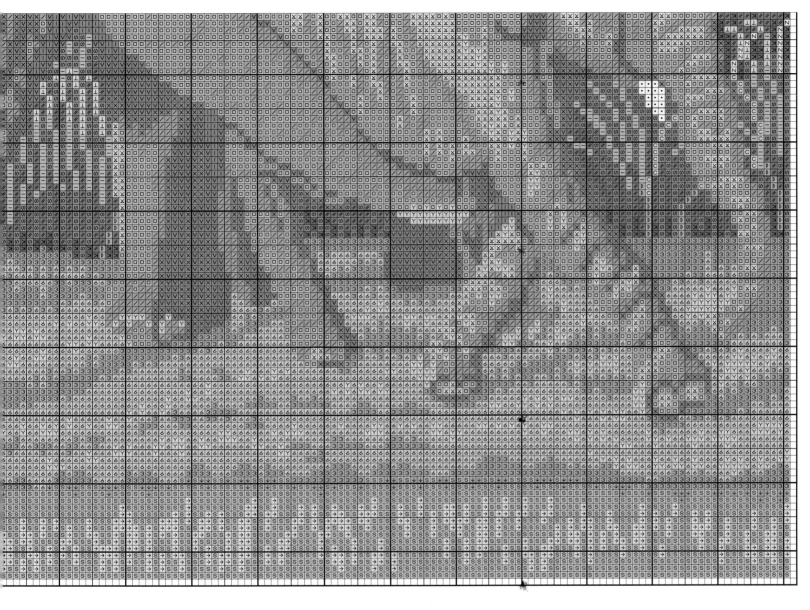

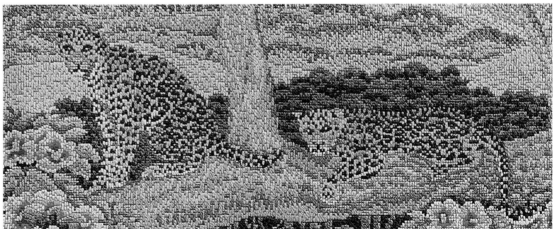

# CACTUS FLOWERS
# CHAIR SEAT

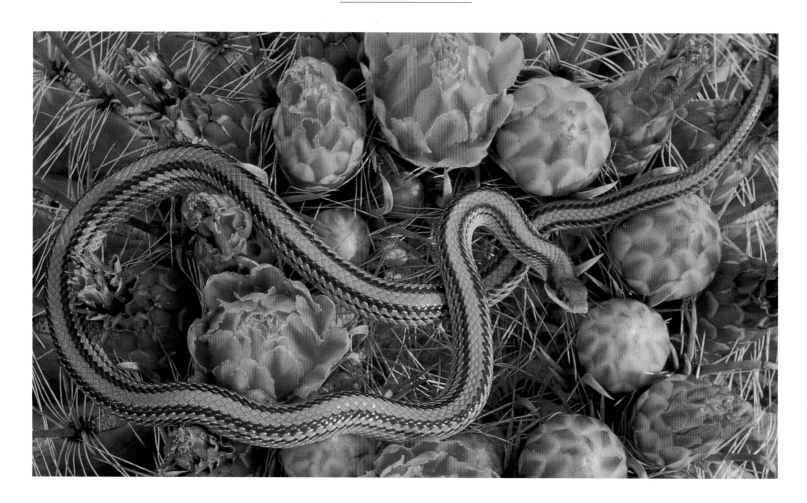

The first surprise for me when looking for interesting cacti was to find that species of cacti grow in all manner of regions, from watery tropical areas to the barest mountain tops, and from regions only slightly above sea level where salt mists moisten them, to the driest deserts with scarcely any rainfall. Less than 10 per cent of cacti live in regions that can truly be classified as deserts, even though most of us associate them with such areas. Whether you would find these species of cacti growing in the same area is rather doubtful, although they do all originate from Mexico.

*ABOVE: The complementary colours of a western patch-nosed snake semi-coiled in the midst of a desert cactus (Bruce Coleman Limited/John Cancalosi).*

While looking at these plants, I had the greatest difficulty choosing which ones to stitch. I knew that there were many beautiful species of cacti but I had not realized before just how many, so I have made notes for lots of future needlepoints. The appeal of many cacti is their strange shapes and textures. Some are barrel shaped, some squat, fat and smooth like strange stones, while others more closely resemble vines or weeping trees. Most cacti have some kind of spine but these also vary greatly. Cacti flowers are usually vivid and often extremely short-lived. I've always thought it rather poignant that some species of cacti only flower once every five years and their one bloom lasts only for a night.

### MATERIALS

CANVAS:

*1 piece, gauge size 10; measuring 52.5 x 50cm (21 x 20in), which allows for a 5cm (2in) surround for stretching*

*Actual size of work: 42.5cm (17in) wide at the front, tapering to 35cm (14in) wide at the back, and (40cm (16in) deep*

PATERNA YARNS:

*White 261*

*Old Gold 755*

*Daffodil 763*

*Autumn Yellow 727*

*Copper 862*

*Earth Brown 413 (2)*

*Toast Brown 471 (3)*

*Mustard 712*

*Plum 322 (2) and 325 (3)*

*Fuchsia 353 and 354 (4)*

*American Beauty 905*

*Hot Pink 962 (2)*

*Flesh 494*

*Strawberry 955, 954 and 952*

*Antique Rose D234 (2)*

*Cranberry 942*

*Teal Blue 523 (3) and 520*

*Pine Green 662 (2)*

*CACTUS FLOWERS*
*CHAIR SEAT KEY*

| | |
|---|---|
| ● | 261 |
| V | 755 |
| = | 763 |
| ∷ | 727 |
| N | 712 |
| ↓ | 862 |
| X | 413 |
| ⌐ | 471 |
| ／ | 322 |
| K | 353 |
| T | 325 |
| ∥ | 354 |
| Z | 905 |
| Y | 962 |
| P | 494 |
| – | 955 |
| U | 954 |
| C | D234 |
| 3 | 952 |
| W | 942 |
| L | 523 |
| ← | 662 |
| ⊓ | 520 |

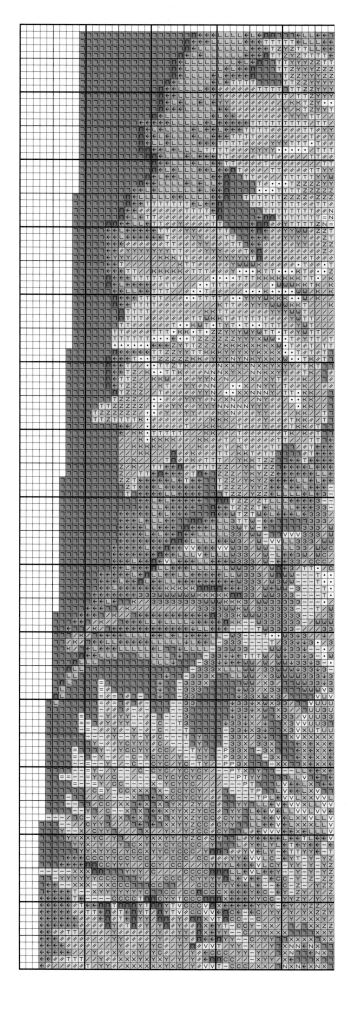

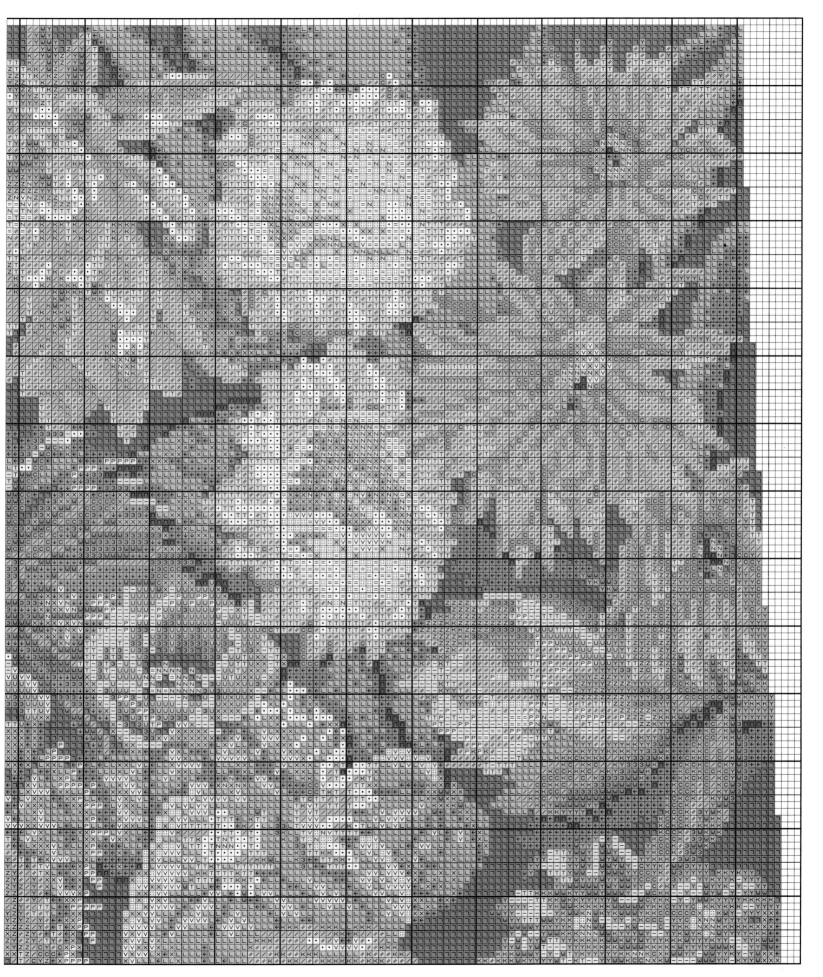

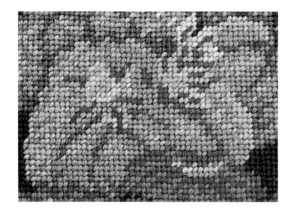

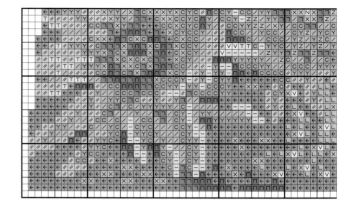

I have tried to keep the colours of the needlepoint within reasonable bounds to make reading the charts easier, but if you feel inspired to use this idea for your own design, you will be amazed at just how many colours you can include. If you grow your own cacti, you will also find interesting design ideas in the patterns that groups of plants form when growing together.

Stitch the design in tent stitch using two threads of yarn throughout *(see page 138)*. Tent stitch is used because it is a very durable, hardwearing stitch, as opposed to half cross stitch or random long stitch. When you have completed the stitching, stretch the canvas and make up the chair seat *(see page 140)*. If you would like to adapt the design to fit your chair, or make the design up into a cushion, see page 140.

# GARDENS INSIDE OUT

---

*The idea of looking out through a window to
a view of a garden beyond, or looking into a room
from outside, opens up new dimensions in
design and offers great potential for needlepoints.*

$\mathrm{D}$istances and dimensions are themes that
interest me greatly, both in needlepoint design and in painting. I love seeing different
dimensions being expressed on a flat surface, being in one room and looking out through
a door or window to another dimension. I particularly like Bonnard's paintings through
doorways and windows because although you get the sense of distance, the colours
outside are no less dramatic than the ones inside. It is easy to wax lyrical over these
paintings as the colours are so glowing and rich.

It is more unusual now to have illustrative needlepoints but in earlier times,
needlepoints and embroideries served as an interesting record of peoples' houses and

gardens. Needlework was not just a hobby to be fitted in at odd times but often a pastime that could be pursued at any hour of the day.

Larger needlepoint hangings came into being initially as a cheaper alternative to the much more expensive woven tapestries, and then became popular in their own right because they could be worked by members of the family rather than by being designed by craftsmen and then sent away, usually to France, to be woven. Nowadays, most stitching enthusiasts prefer a work size that is portable and can be finished in a reasonable period of time, so these smaller pictorial needlepoints can serve as miniature wall hangings or interesting pillows. The pieces in this chapter are both worked in random long stitch but would work equally well in tent stitch.

*ABOVE: A sunken pool set in a courtyard, with topiary and a pillared summer house (The Garden Picture Library / John Glover).*

# SUNKEN POOL PILLOW

This design is stitched in subtle, muted shades to form a contrast with the following pillow and to show the difference in effect that the two colours make. The idea for this needlepoint came from looking at sunken pools in courtyards surrounded by pot plants and fruit trees, coupled with a desire to echo the pool in the sunken garden at Packwood House which was stitched for the other pillow. I also thought it would be interesting to be able to see into a room and then on through a window to the view beyond. This gives the design more depth; when working on fairly large-gauge canvas on a small area, it is often difficult to include enough detail and therefore enough depth in the design, so adding depth to the visual content is one way of resolving this.

I worked this design on double-threaded canvas and, in theory, it would have been possible to have split the threads and used twice as many stitches. This would have been difficult to chart for this design, but it is an option to remember when designing for yourself. It is easier to use twice as many stitches if using tent stitch rather than random long stitch, and it means that you can choose certain detailed areas for the *petit point* while still stitching the bulk of the design in the larger tent stitch, or *gros point*. This technique was often employed as a means of stitching faces or entire figures in earlier needlepoint pieces.

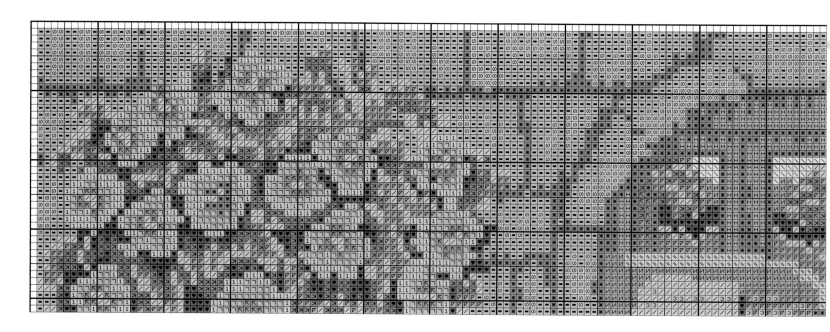

## MATERIALS

CANVAS:

*1 piece, gauge size 10, measuring 70 x 55cm (28 x 22in), which allows a 5cm (2in) surround for stretching*

*Actual size of work: 60 x 45cm (24 x 18in)*

PATERNA YARNS:

*Loden Green 692 (4), 693 (5) and 694 (3)*

*Khaki Green 643 (6) and 644 (3)*

*Hunter Green 611 (3) and 612 (2)*

*Teal Blue 522 (4) and 523*

*Caribbean Blue 595*

*Blue Spruce 533*

*Toast Brown 472 (2)*

*Marigold 803*

*Golden Brown 443 (3)*

*Hot Pink 964, 963 (2) and 962*

*Tangerine 825*

*Plum 325*

*Beige Brown 462 (4)*

*Cinnamon D411 and D419 (2)*

*Coffee Brown 423 (2)*

*Bittersweet 833 (2)*

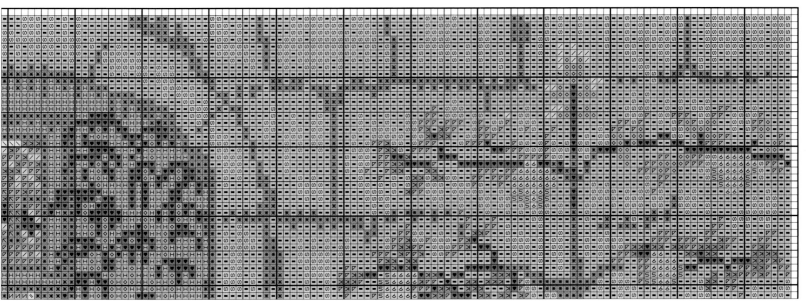

*SUNKEN POOL PILLOW KEY*

| | |
|---|---|
| □ 964 | 5 833 |
| ⊓ 962 | 6 803 |
| 1 963 | H 443 |
| 3 825 | L 325 |
| + 423 | ▼ D411 |

| | |
|---|---|
| ∧ D419 | ▼ 611 |
| ✳ 462 | ▽ 693 |
| ⊾ 472 | ╱ 694 |
| ⊿ 692 | ╲ 595 |
| ◇ 612 | ⋈ 522 |

| |
|---|
| ● 533 |
| ∥ 523 |
| ■ 643 |
| S 644 |

Stitch the canvas in random long stitch, using two threads of yarn throughout *(see page 138)*. When the stitching is finished, the piece will need to be stretched and made up into a pillow *(see page 139)*.

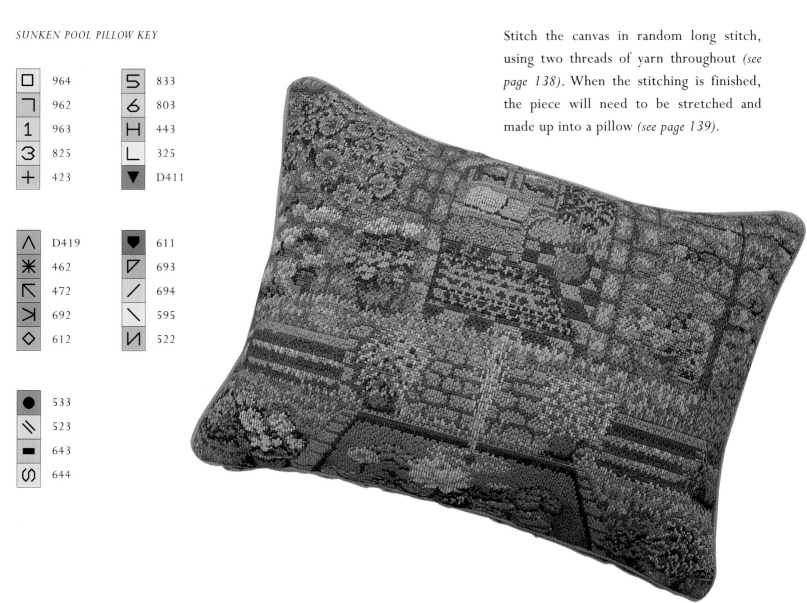

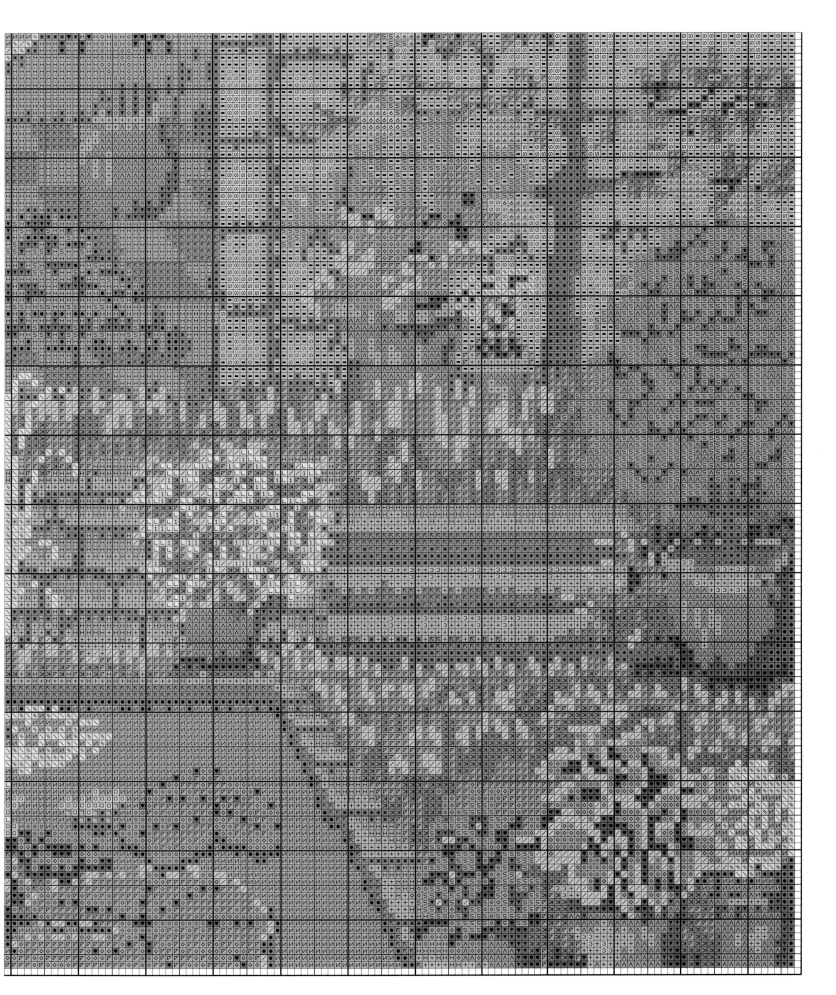

# GARDEN VIEW PILLOW

The gardens of stately homes and country houses are a living library of needlepoint designs. Within these gardens are many of the styles and characteristics of the past 300 to 400 years, in addition to a tremendously varied collection of plants.

This design looks out through an archway into the sunken garden of Packwood House, a 16th-century house in Warwickshire, well known for its giant yew trees which can be seen in this needlepoint beyond the wall of the garden. There are scores of yew trees in this garden, clipped as giant cones and tapering cylinders, some reaching 6m (20ft) in height. It has been widely thought for many years that the original 13 yews were intended to represent the Sermon on the Mount, with the large single yew tree – the Master – standing alone on the mount, and the 12 great yews on the cross walk representing the Apostles.

*ABOVE: The sunken pool at Packwood House in Warwickshire*

*(National Trust Photographic Library / Richard Surman).*

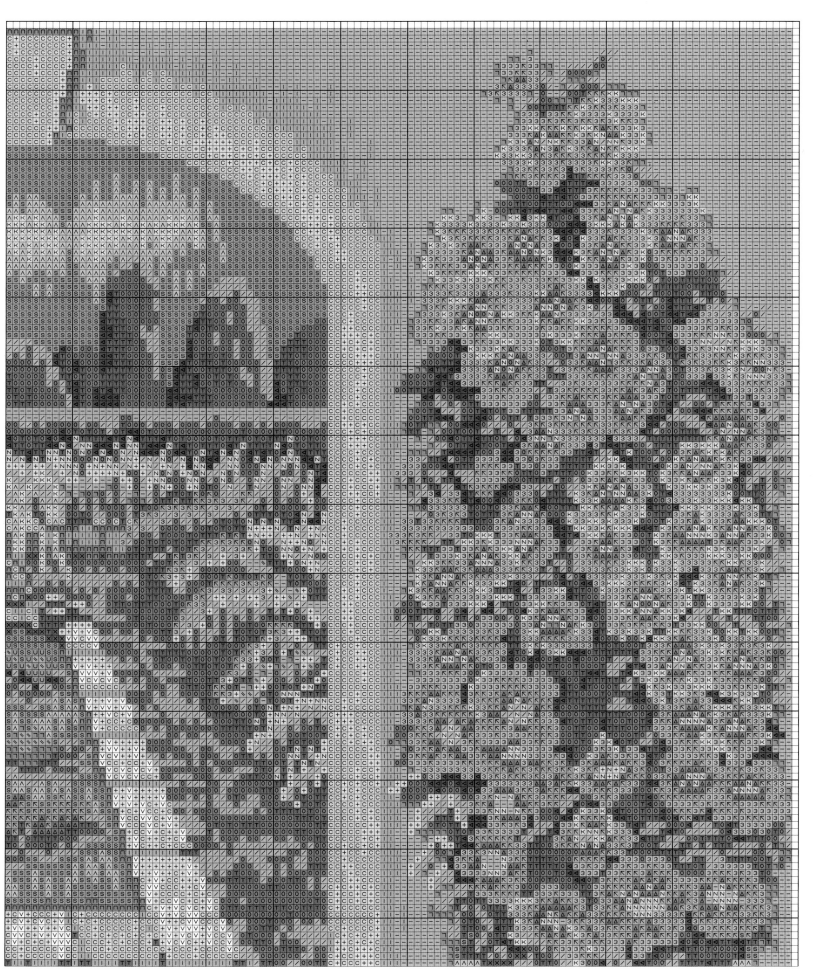

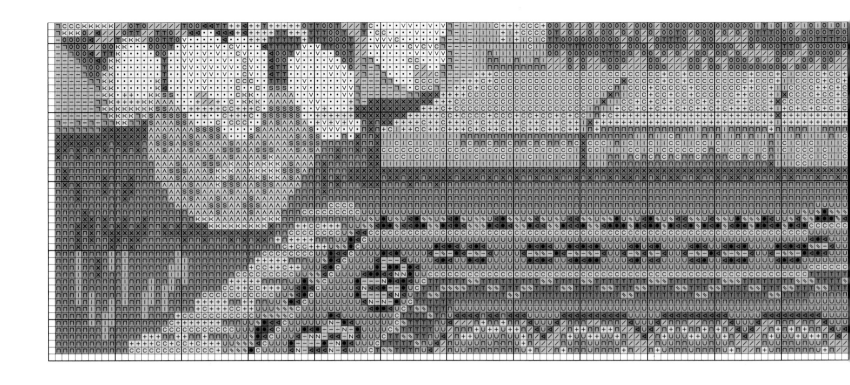

## MATERIALS

**CANVAS:**

*1 piece, gauge size 10;*

*measuring 70 x 55cm (28 x 22in),*

*which allows a 5cm (2in) surround*

*for stretching*

*Actual size of work:*

*60 x 45cm (24 x 18in)*

**PATERNA YARNS:**

*White 261*

*Hot Pink 962 (2) and 963 (2)*

*Salmon 842 (2)*

*Cranberry 942*

*Tangerine 825*

*Copper 863 (9) and 862*

*Bittersweet 832 (4)*

*Mustard 712*

*Olive Green 654 (2), 653 (5) and 650*

*Khaki Green 642 (2) and 643 (2)*

*Loden Green 690 (2), 691 (3), 692 (4),*

*   693 (3) and 694 (3)*

*Blue Spruce 531*

*Cool Grey 236 (2)*

*Federal Blue 505 (2)*

*Ice Blue 553 (3)*

Inside the room of the needlepoint, there is a bowl of white tulips, a climbing rose, and a copy of my flamingo tapestry from *The Tapestry Book.* I enjoyed stitching this needlepoint in miniature enormously. It was quite a challenge to make it recognizable and to convey the actual feeling that the piece has. Stitch the canvas in random long stitch, using two threads of yarn throughout *(see page 138)*. When the stitching is complete, stretch the canvas and make it up into a pillow *(see page 139)*. Alternatively, you could make it up into a small hanging if you prefer *(see page 141)*.

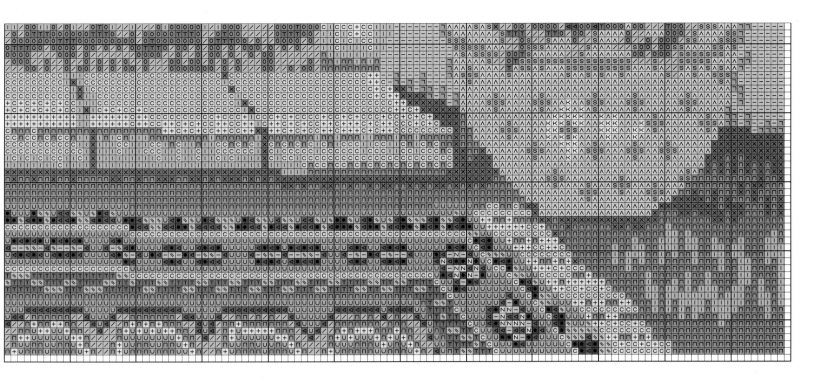

## GARDEN VIEW PILLOW KEY

| | | | | |
|---|---|---|---|---|
| ● | 261 | I | | 643 |
| 3 | 963 | ⊓ | X | 642 |
| ⊏ | 962 | X | | 650 |
| U | 842 | + | | 694 |
| △ | 942 | ∕ | | 693 |
| ∖ | 825 | O | | 692 |
| ⌐ | 863 | T | | 691 |
| ⌐ | 832 | ◁ | | 690 |
| ⌐ | 862 | ● | | 531 |
| N | 712 | K | | 236 |
| V | 654 | ∧ | | 505 |
| C | 653 | S | | 553 |

# WATER WILDLIFE

*Water — whether in ponds, streams or waterfalls*
*— and the wildlife it nurtures are two of*
*my favourite themes; between them, they offer*
*an abundance of subjects to depict in wool.*

Although I now live a long way from the sea, I don't live far from water. I cannot hear the sound of waves crashing on the beach, but every day I can listen to the stream nearby running over the stones and cascading in little waterfalls. Occasionally it becomes a roaring torrent and is unrecognizable as the friendly little stream that I paddle in and sit by, the same one that the children spend hours in catching all kinds of fish, examining them and letting them go again. I see both herons and frogs here and, on lucky days, I catch a brief glimpse of the kingfisher.

One year, when it rained much more than usual, and the stream had flooded its banks, we had frogs hopping everywhere. I don't know whether it was too wet even for them, but we found them leaping into every outbuilding and even trying to get into the house. It's a good thing we all like frogs!

I am continually overwhelmed by the ideas for designs that come from water and its associated wildlife. The two designs in this chapter were chosen because they show two very different views of water wildlife. I associate the Grey Heron Cushion particularly with English pond and stream life, whereas the Frog and Lilies Cushion uses the hotter colours of tropical regions.

There are so many aspects of wildlife and the countryside just waiting to be stitched, that I now have lots more ideas for needlepoint designs. At present many species of wildlife are rarely seen, and some are actually in danger of becoming extinct. Nowadays, I don't often see many of the creatures I frequently saw as a child, particularly deer, otters and grass snakes. Perhaps by stitching a small part of our wildlife we will remember to value it even more than we do already.

# GREY HERON CUSHION

This was the first design that I sketched for the book, as the grey heron constantly reminds me of its existence. There are three herons that fly around my house, occasionally all together, and I think they are a pair with their young one. But it is usually the largest one that I see in the early mornings if I am very quiet; he stands immobile on the bridge, watching and waiting to decide which side of the stream to go in that day. Inevitably, I have never managed to photograph him – he always flies away as I tiptoe to get my camera.

Seeing and hearing the grey herons flying is quite extraordinary. Their cries to each other are so loud and sound so prehistoric. They fly with their necks bent, their heads drawn back and their legs trailing. Like this, they remind you strongly of their ancient ancestors, the pterodactyls, as they fly over.

I find it interesting, as with the snow geese, that although herons appear to be quite muted in colour, once you really start looking at them as you must do when you are going to do a design from them, they have so many different shades of pastel white and charcoal black that my stitching palette is quite large.

The water and the mossy stones in this design are taken from sketches I've drawn and painted of the stream and surrounding hills around my home. In fact, designing this cushion provided me with wonderful justification for sitting in my favourite spot by the stream. I had a lot of fun stitching the water and making it flow over and between the mossy rocks.

| | |
|---|---|
| ● | 260 |
| P | 261 |
| U | 725 |
| I | 722 |
| + | 720 |
| ✳ | 694 |
| O | 693 |
| C | 692 |
| Δ | 691 |
| ⋋ | 690 |
| ⅃ | 652 |
| ⌐ | 651 |
| ∧ | 650 |
| = | 585 |
| ⊼ | D392 |
| ⋌ | D391 |
| ● | D389 |
| | D346 |
| ● | 221 |

## MATERIALS

CANVAS:

*1 piece, gauge size 10; measuring 50 x 50cm
(20 x 20in), which allows for a 5cm (2in)
surround for stretching*

*Actual size of work: 40 x 40cm (16 x 16in)*

PATERNA YARNS:

*Charcoal 221*

*Dolphin D346, D389, D391 and D392 (3)*

*Olive Green 650 (2), 651 (2) and 652 (2)*

*Loden Green 690 (2), 691 (3), 692 (3), 693 (3)
and 694 (2)*

*Autumn Yellow 720, 722 and 725*

*White 260 (2)*

*Off White 261 (4)*

*Sky Blue 585 (2)*

Stitch the canvas in tent stitch, using two
threads of yarn throughout *(see page 138)*.
When the stitching is complete, stretch the
canvas and make it up into a cushion *(see
page 139)*.

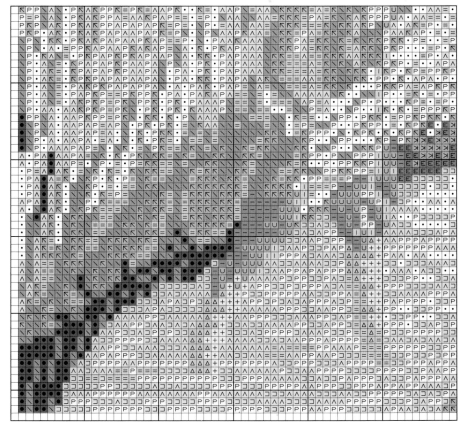

You will see from the close-up here how the effect of water trickling down through mossy rocks is achieved. It is quite difficult to see whether you are being successful as you stitch — which is why I invariably keep pinning my work up so that I can look at it from a distance, to make sure that I am getting the effect I want.

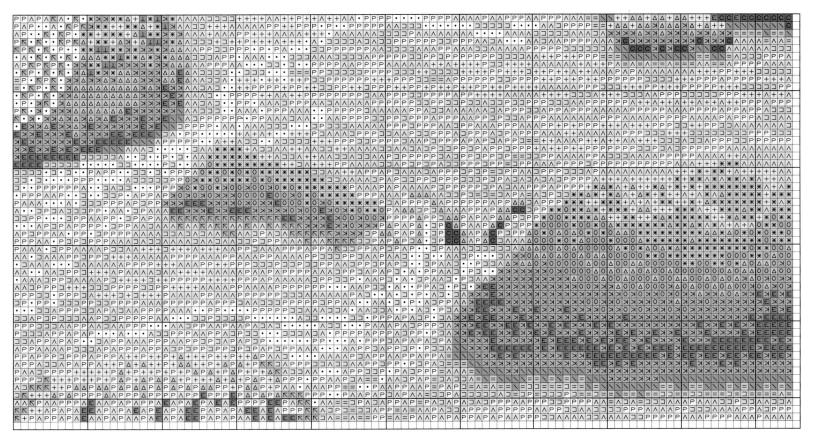

# FROG AND LILIES CUSHION

Giant water lily pads seem unbelievably big to me, probably because we are accustomed to our small native water lilies. The Amazon Basin's royal water lily, *Victoria amazonica*, certainly is giant. The leaves spread to 2m (7ft) wide and are supported by air-filled ribs which make them buoyant enough to bear a child's weight. The beautiful terracotta-coloured rim of the leaf has spiny edges which deter most herbivores. Unfortunately, the lakes in the Amazon, where these lilies often grow, are a favourite dwelling place of piranha fish, so one would want to be fairly sure of their weight-supporting ability before hopping on to find out.

The nearest I have come to these wonderful plants is seeing them at Kew Gardens in London. Although there is a limited space at Kew, one can still visualize what these giant water lilies must look like *en masse* in South America. Their flowers too

are on a giant scale and are wonderfully plump before they burst into bloom.

The frog stitched here is the moor frog, which actually lives in northern Europe, Scandinavia and Siberia, so he's well off course in this design! He hibernates in mud during the winter and then he turns this lovely bluish-turquoise colour in the breeding season.

*RIGHT: The giant leaves of the royal water lily,* Victoria amazonica, *spread to 2m (7ft) wide (Michelle Garrett).*

## MATERIALS

CANVAS:

*1 piece, gauge size 10; measuring 50 x 50cm (20 x 20in), which allows for a 5cm (2in) surround for stretching*

*Actual size of work: 40 x 40cm (16 x 16in)*

PATERNA YARNS:

*Rusty Rose 934*

*Antique Rose D275 (2) and D234*

*Hot Pink 962 (2)*

*American Beauty 903*

*Copper 863*

*Verdigris D531 (2)*

*Charcoal 221*

*Loden Green 692 (2), 693 (3) and 694 (2)*

*Hunter Green 610 (3) and 612 (3)*

*Blue Spruce 533 (4)*

*Teal Blue 522 (3)*

*Seafarer D503*

*Cobalt Blue 546*

Stitch the canvas in tent stitch, using two threads of yarn throughout *(see page 138)*. When the stitching is complete, stretch the canvas and make it up into a cushion *(see page 139)*.

*FROG AND LILIES*

*CUSHION KEY*

| Symbol | Color |
|--------|-------|
| I | 934 |
| — | D275 |
| L | D234 |
| Y | 962 |
| ∕∕ | 903 |
| U | 863 |
| C | D531 |
| ◇ | 694 |
| + | 693 |
| Z | 692 |
| Q | 612 |
| ∧ | 610 |
| X | 533 |
| 6 | 522 |
| \ | D503 |
| ◁ | 546 |
| S | 221 |

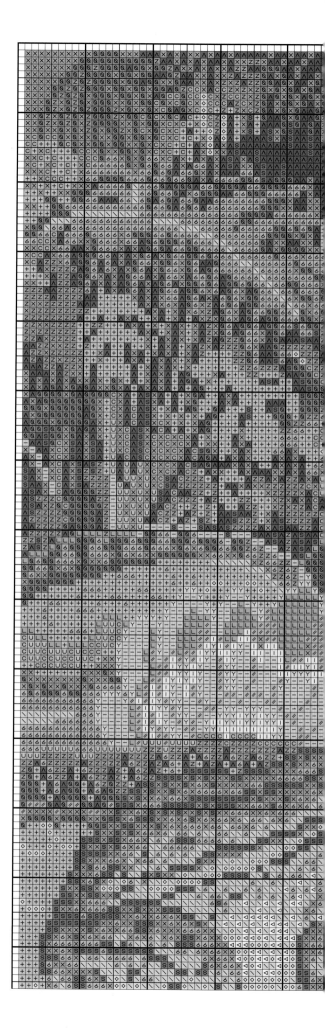

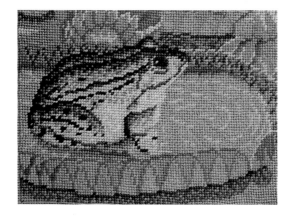

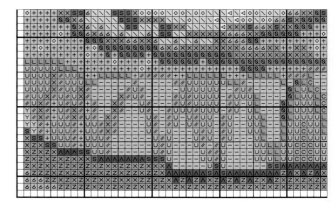

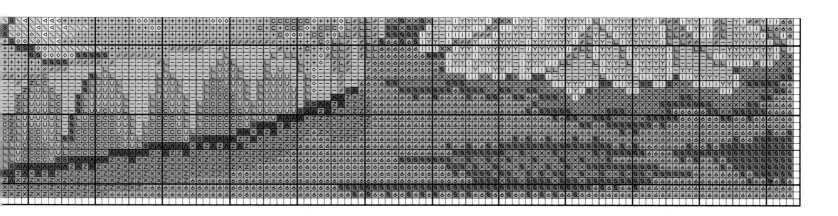

# MATERIALS

One of the joys of needlepoint is being able to carry all the equipment you need
for a wonderful tapestry around with you. All you need are the canvas,
yarns, a needle and a pair of scissors. Everything else is an optional extra.

### CANVAS

The three main types of canvas to choose
from are mono (single thread), interlock
and double thread (or Penelope). If you use
single-thread canvas, you must be sure to do
tent stitch, not half cross stitch, which will
unravel on this type of canvas (see Techniques).

All the designs in this book, except for
one, are worked on double-thread canvas of
gauge size 10, which means that there are 10
stitches to every 2.5cm (1in). The exception
is the poppy screen which is worked on
double-thread canvas with 7.6 holes to
every 2.5cm (1in) and is therefore quicker
to work.

There are many different colours of
canvas available. My preference is for
antique colour double-thread canvas. It suits
the stitches I use, which are tent stitch and
random long stitch. It is a very sympathetic
colour to design on and much easier on the
eye than glaring white, and it does not show
through your finished stitches.

*A detailed shot of the Poppy Screen
in which you can see clearly how the stitches
add life and texture to the flowers.*

### YARNS

Throughout this book I have used Paterna
Persian yarns because I love their brilliant
transparent colours, and I like the quality of
the thread. This comes in three threads
which are loosely twisted together to make
one strand but they can be separated easily.
All the designs except for the poppy screen
use two threads of yarn. (When separating
off the third thread, save it to combine with
the next extra thread so that no yarn is
wasted.) Keys for the threads are given with
each chart. Where more than one skein is
needed to complete a design, the number of
skeins is given after each appropriate thread
number in the list of materials. You could
use alternative yarn if you prefer (see the
conversion table on page 142), but the finished
results will not be as vibrant as my original
pieces, as the colours do not match exactly.

### NEEDLES

Use proper tapestry needles for
needlepoint. They have a rounded point so
that you do not continually stab yourself or
snag the canvas. They come in many
different sizes. For the gauge size 7.6
canvas, I use a size 18 needle and for the
gauge size 10, I use a size 20 needle, but it
does not matter which you use as long as the
needle passes through the canvas easily and
pleasantly.

# TECHNIQUES

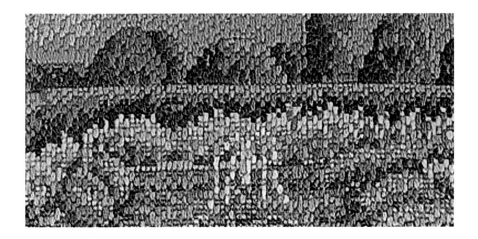

## PREPARATION

The canvas should be cut approximately 5cm (2in) larger all the way round than the size of the actual finished work. This allows a margin for stretching the piece back to its original proportions. The process of stitching distorts the canvas to some extent – much more so when tent stitch is used, because of its diagonal pull. But random long stitch also looks neater and more finished once it has been stretched back to shape.

When cutting your canvas, always cut exactly along one thread otherwise the canvas will unravel. Before stitching, it is useful to bind the edges with masking tape or turn the raw edges under and quickly hem them; this prevents the yarn from catching on them while you are stitching.

Make sure that throughout the process of stitching, the top of the canvas is identifiable in some way. This will safeguard against you resuming work after an interruption, only to start stitching in the opposite direction.

Use lengths of yarn measuring up to 50cm (20in); anything longer will become weak and thin, leaving areas of canvas exposed between the stitches.

It is important to avoid using knots, since they create a lumpy texture and make it hard to stretch the work evenly. Make the first stitch so that with your other hand you are holding a 7.5cm (3in) length of yarn firmly on the underside of the canvas. Keep holding this tail of thread while you pull the first stitch firm; then continue so that the next few stitches are worked over the loose yarn on the wrong side, making it invisible. The same effect can be achieved when finishing off, by darning the remains of the thread under the stitching and cutting off any remainder.

One of the major debates of needlepoint is whether or not to work with a frame. All I can say is, please stitch in whichever way makes you comfortable and gives you the most pleasure. The advantage of using a frame is that it keeps the work stretched and the correct tension. The drawback of not working on a frame is that the finished piece needs more stretching unless your tension is very good – and it is possible to get it very good. The advantage of not working with a frame is portability and speed and the fact that it is much easier to design on the canvas without the limitations of a frame.

## USING CHARTS

The charts in this book are extremely easy to work from as they are in full colour and include symbols as well, enabling you to photocopy or enlarge a chart if necessary. Each square on the chart represents a single stitch. Where the chart is for a project that has been worked in random long stitch, choose the length of stitch you would like; I suggest keeping the maximum length to covering four horizontal pairs of threads. When you are actually stitching, you will soon get used to choosing the length of your stitches when it is an area of one colour to be filled in.

Before you start to stitch, familiarize yourself with the wool colours and the symbols that represent them by putting the wools on to a punched-hole cardboard organizer, with the numbers and symbols written beside them.

NEEDLEPOINT STITCHES

At present, the only stitches I use in my work are tent stitch and random long stitch. This is because my main interest lies in what you can convey in colour and line, and, for me, different textured stitches are an unnecessary complication. I use tent stitch in preference to half cross stitch because it is extremely hardwearing and produces a more substantial textile.

*Tent stitch* is worked diagonally over only one intersection of the canvas. The needle always covers at least two threads on the wrong side of the work.

*Continental tent stitch* is worked from right to left along the first row, then back along the next row from left to right.

*Basketweave tent stitch* is worked diagonally from top left to bottom right, taking the needle over one intersection of the canvas and covering two threads behind the work. Then the second row comes back from bottom right to top left, in between the first stitches to create a woven effect. The third row repeats the first row, so the stitches are worked in between the stitches of the second row, and so on.

*Half cross stitch* is worked from left to right on the first row, then back along the next row from right to left. The needle goes over one intersection of canvas, and covers one thread on the back of the work.

**Continental tent stitch**

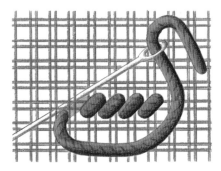

**Basketweave tent stitch**

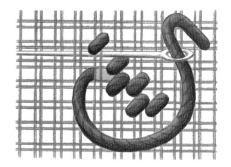

**Half cross stitch**

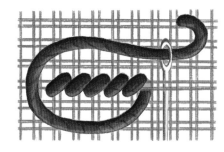
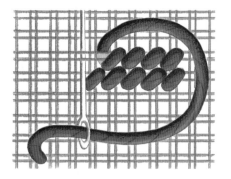

**Random long stitch**

*Random long stitch* is a straight stitch which lies parallel to the canvas threads. It is ideal for filling large areas of canvas quickly, as it is worked in varying lengths along each row. It is worked row by row, alternating from left to right then from right to left, with the rows interlocking. When I work random long stitch, I take care to cover the back as well as the front, by using a circular motion when stitching. It is better not to have too many stitches going over just one pair of threads in the canvas as this tends to leave canvas showing.

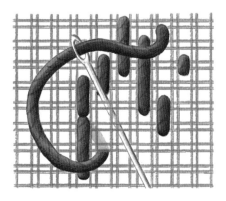

## STRETCHING OR BLOCKING

When you have finished stitching the needlepoint, you will need to stretch your work. This means pulling it and stretching it gently back into its original dimensions. There are two ways of doing this. One way is to make a template of the original dimensions of the canvas from brown paper or thin cardboard, then place the template on top of the stitched canvas and pull the canvas out to the edges of the template. Alternatively you can use a set square for the corners and use a metal ruler or piece of wood to straighten the edges.

In either case, you will need to find a piece of particle wood or similar board, suitable for hammering 5cm (2in) nails into. For ease of use, the board should be at least 7.5cm (3in) larger all the way round than the canvas you intend to stretch. Cover the board with a sheet of clean cartridge paper or clean undyed material, the same size or larger than the needlepoint, then place the needlepoint face down on top of it. Dampen the wrong side of the canvas with a flower mister or a sponge. Now, using your

template or a set square, start pulling the canvas gently back into shape. I find it easiest first to line up one edge with the straight side of the board and secure that side with a few nails, then to start straightening the other three sides, using a set square to make sure the right angles are true. Once the measurements are correct, hammer in nails around the edges until they are suitably straight and the whole piece is nailed at about 2.5cm (1in) intervals.

Brush wallpaper paste evenly over the back of the canvas to size it. This helps the work to retain its shape. Leave it to dry naturally in a warm, dry place for at least 48 hours or until it is completely dry. The nails can be pulled out with a claw hammer or pliers and the work is then ready to be made up.

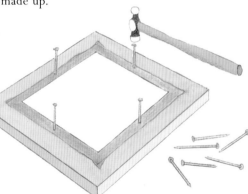

*Stretch the needlepoint over the board, holding it in place by lightly hammering a nail midway down each side.*

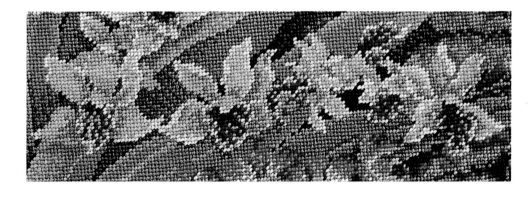

## CUSHIONS AND PILLOWS

To make a cushion or pillow, choose a backing fabric that complements the colours of the needlepoint, especially if you are going to use it to make piping. If you intend to do this, be sure to buy extra backing material.

Use the finished needlepoint as a guide for cutting the backing fabric, adding a further 1.5cm (⅝in) all around for a seam allowance.

If you wish to use a zip fastener, cut the piece in two, adding an extra seam allowance on each half for the zip. Insert the zip in the centre back seam by stitching the top and the bottom and basting the remainder. Insert the zip in the basted part of the seam and machine in the zip.

Then, with the right sides together, pin the backing to the needlepoint. Machine stitch this as close to the needlepoint as possible along all four edges, or three if you are not using a zip. Trim the needlepoint canvas and the seam allowance and cut diagonally across the corners, taking care not to cut the stitching. Turn the cushion cover the right way out and insert the cushion pad. Feather cushion pads give the best effect and it is a good idea to use a slightly larger pad than the dimensions of the cushion. This gives a pleasantly plump feel to the cushion. Zip up the cushion cover, or slipstitch the fourth edge by hand.

*Place the needlepoint right side down on a board, then dampen it by spraying with a mister or dabbing with a sponge.*

## ADAPTING A CHAIR SEAT DESIGN

To adapt a chair seat design into a cushion, simply make the design 40cm (16in) square instead of the shape of the chair seat. Mark the centre line of your canvas as you would for the cushion but then work exactly 80 stitches to each side of that line. This means that at the bottom of the work you will need to add stitches in the background colour and at the top you will need to omit an equal number of stitches from each side.

## BOX CUSHIONS

Use the finished needlepoint as a guide for cutting out the bottom panel of the box cushion, adding a further 1.5cm (⅝in) all around for a seam allowance. The border should measure 7.5cm (3in) wide and should equal the length of the four sides of the needlepoint; if possible, cut this in one piece, adding a 1.5cm (⅝in) seam allowance to each side. Stitch the short ends together, right sides facing.

If you wish to include a zip, stitch it to the bottom panel of the cushion, following the instructions for Cushions and Pillows above. Then machine stitch the border to the bottom panel, with right sides together, leaving a 30cm (12in) opening to insert the cushion pad. Machine the border to the needlepoint, right sides together. Notch the four corners of the border. Turn the cushion cover the right side out. Insert the cushion pad, then slipstitch the gap to close.

## PIPING

Edging a cushion or pillow with piping cord adds a stylish finishing touch. It is very easy to cover piping cord with complementary fabric. Simply cut bias strips of fabric wide enough to cover the cord plus a seam allowance of 12mm (½in) on each side. You might have to join strips of fabric to make the required length; if so, press the seams of the join open before covering the cord. Fold the strips around the piping cord and baste into place close to the cord. Then pin the piping to the right side of the needlepoint so that the raw edges of the piping and the canvas are matching. Then pin and baste the backing fabric over the needlepoint, sandwiching the piping, and machine in place. Clip the corners diagonally and turn the cushion cover the right way out.

If adding piping to a box cushion, sew the piping to the top border edge before joining it to the bottom panel.

## CHAIR SEATS

Stretch the finished piece back to its original dimensions of 42.5 x 35 x 40cm (17 x 14 x 16in). Trim the canvas, leaving 4.5cm (1¾in) around the edge of the stitching. Stitch a double row of stitches around the outside edge of the trimmed canvas. Then stitch a gathering thread around the canvas, between the finished piece and the double row of stitches. Put the needlepoint face down on a clean cloth and position the chair seat pad face down on top of it, making sure that it is centred. Pull the gathering thread up, making sure that the design is positioned correctly on the pad. Then baste or staple the canvas on to the hard underside of the seat pad and place the seat pad on to the chair.

You can enlarge the size of the chair seat design to fit your chair by drawing out the larger seat dimensions on to your canvas. Then simply continue the background colours on around the edges, provided it is not for too many extra holes. Remember to allow 5cm (2in) extra canvas around the finished work size, for stretching. In the same way, you can make the design area smaller by stitching less of the design, ensuring that you decrease stitches equally from each side of the design.

## ADAPTING A CUSHION DESIGN

To adapt a cushion design to make a chair seat, mark your canvas with the centre line of the design, then mark on the dimensions for the chair seat above (or the dimensions of your own chair seat if they are different). Then add more stitches of the cushion design at the top, and stitch less at the bottom, to fill the area of the chair seat.

WALL HANGINGS

To make an unframed wall hanging, mitre the corners of the finished canvas by first trimming off the excess canvas around the edges, leaving about 3cm (1¼in) all around. With the wrong side facing, fold each corner diagonally towards the centre of the canvas, and press. Then fold in the other two edges of each corner and stitch neatly along the diagonal seam. Secure the edges on the back with herringbone stitch.

*Mitre the corners as for a hanging and then hold in place round the filler by lacing the sides together.*

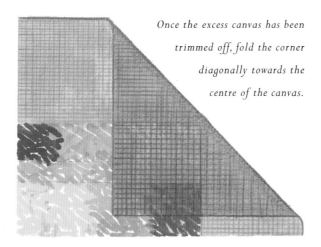

*Once the excess canvas has been trimmed off, fold the corner diagonally towards the centre of the canvas.*

*Fold down the other two edges and stitch neatly along the diagonal seam to hold in place.*

The wall hanging can then be backed with upholstery fabric. Cut a piece of fabric the same size as the hanging, plus a 1.5cm (⅝in) seam allowance all around. With right sides facing, machine the backing fabric to the two long sides and the shorter bottom edge of the wall hanging. If you are going to use a rod to hang it, stop machining 5cm (2in) before the top of the piece which will leave a gap large enough to feed the rod through. Turn the hanging the right side out and firmly slipstitch the top edge to the backing fabric, turning under the seam allowance. Thread the rod through and hang the wall hanging by resting the rod on cup hooks or by attaching braid to the rod and hanging the braid from picture hooks.

FIRESCREENS

To mount a firescreen, place the stretched needlepoint centrally on the filler panel. You can then either pull the canvas edges round to the back and lace them together tightly enough to keep the needlepoint taut, or trim the canvas edges to an appropriate length and staple the work on to the filler board with a staple gun. The filler is then put into the frame and held in place by the backing board of the screen.

POPPY SCREEN

Mount this in the same way as the firescreen for all three panels.

# CONVERSION TABLE

The tapestries in this book have all been stitched with Paterna yarns. This table suggests DMC and Anchor yarns in shades comparable to the Paterna yarn numbers. However, as the shades of the yarns produced by the three companies differ quite widely, the apppearance of the finished tapestries will be affected if alternative yarns are used.

| Paterna | DMC | Anchor | Paterna | DMC | Anchor | Paterna | DMC | Anchor | Paterna | DMC | Anchor |
|---|---|---|---|---|---|---|---|---|---|---|---|
| 210 | 7713 | 8720 | 523 | 7323 | 8934 | 693 | 7548 | 9196 | 875 | 7191 | 9612 |
| 211 | 7284 | 8718 | 525 | 7322 | 8912 | 694 | 7549 | 9212 | 883 | 7919 | 9556 |
| 212 | 7282 | 8714 | 531 | 7327 | 8884 | 695 | 7351 | 9256 | 886 | 7179 | 9506 |
| 213 | 7715 | 8712 | 533 | 7695 | 8880 | 696 | 7915 | 9120 | 900 | 7219 | 8426 |
| 221 | 7624 | 9798 | 542 | 7797 | 8690 | 702 | 7783 | 8098 | 901 | 7210 | 8404 |
| 236 | 7510 | 8702 | 543 | 7995 | 8688 | 711 | 7785 | 8098 | 902 | 7138 | 8402 |
| 256 | 7300 | 9782 | 544 | 7317 | 8672 | 712 | 7726 | 8118 | 903 | 7602 | 8418 |
| 260 | White | 8000 | 545 | 7283 | 8686 | 713 | 7727 | 8116 | 904 | 7603 | 8416 |
| 261 | Ecru | 8002 | 546 | 7301 | 8682 | 720 | 7401 | 9542 | 905 | 7605 | 8452 |
| 263 | Ecru | 8006 | 552 | 7316 | 8690 | 722 | 7445 | 8102 | 913 | 7204 | 8416 |
| 314 | 7709 | 8586 | 553 | 7313 | 8776 | 723 | 7444 | 8100 | 914 | 7211 | 8482 |
| 322 | 7255 | 8526 | 555 | 7301 | 8772 | 724 | 7175 | 8140 | 915 | 7132 | 8394 |
| 325 | 7790 | 8542 | 556 | 7587 | 8812 | 725 | 7506 | 8136 | 931 | 7205 | 8400 |
| 326 | 7132 | 8342 | 563 | 7799 | 8602 | 727 | 7078 | 8056 | 934 | 7132 | 8394 |
| 341 | 7797 | 8644 | 580 | 7311 | 8794 | 732 | 7474 | 8060 | 940 | 7137 | 8442 |
| 342 | 7798 | 8608 | 582 | 7995 | 8808 | 743 | 7503 | 8040 | 941 | 7600 | 8216 |
| 343 | 7711 | 8604 | 583 | 7813 | 8806 | 751 | 7781 | 8044 | 942 | 7640 | 8440 |
| 344 | 7800 | 8602 | 584 | 7996 | 8804 | 752 | 7783 | 8024 | 944 | 7135 | 8436 |
| 353 | 7153 | 8488 | 585 | 7828 | 8802 | 753 | 7473 | 8060 | 950 | 7544 | 8218 |
| 354 | 7151 | 8486 | 592 | 7807 | 8938 | 755 | 7905 | 8052 | 952 | 7135 | 8214 |
| 413 | 7918 | 9446 | 593 | 7598 | 8916 | 760 | 7433 | 8094 | 953 | 7104 | 8212 |
| 414 | 7144 | 9444 | 600 | 7428 | 9022 | 763 | 7745 | 8014 | 954 | 7103 | 8434 |
| 421 | 7489 | 9648 | 610 | 7385 | 9008 | 771 | 7971 | 8120 | 955 | 7103 | 8432 |
| 432 | 7497 | 9428 | 611 | 7320 | 9104 | 773 | 7745 | 8114 | 961 | 7602 | 8456 |
| 440 | 7845 | 9410 | 612 | 7384 | 9102 | 801 | 7740 | 8156 | 962 | 7603 | 8454 |
| 441 | 7513 | 9428 | 632 | 7342 | 9116 | 803 | 7175 | 9554 | 963 | 7804 | 8452 |
| 442 | 7494 | 9426 | 633 | 7341 | 9114 | 805 | 7905 | 9522 | 970 | 7107 | 8202 |
| 443 | 7494 | 9424 | 634 | 7340 | 9154 | 825 | 7179 | 8302 | D115 | 7238 | 9684 |
| 455 | 7411 | 9484 | 642 | 7355 | 9310 | 830 | 7360 | 8236 | D234 | 7759 | 8398 |
| 460 | 7416 | 9662 | 643 | 7423 | 9306 | 832 | 7947 | 8234 | D275 | 7760 | 8368 |
| 461 | 7416 | 9660 | 650 | 7393 | 9314 | 833 | 7214 | 8192 | D346 | 7705 | 9068 |
| 462 | 7413 | 9658 | 651 | 7425 | 9310 | 834 | 7762 | 8232 | D389 | 7285 | 9064 |
| 463 | 7520 | 9656 | 652 | 7363 | 9308 | 835 | 7853 | 8252 | D391 | 7331 | 8706 |
| 464 | 7520 | 9654 | 653 | 7361 | 9258 | 841 | 7666 | 8216 | D392 | 7321 | 8704 |
| 471 | 7236 | 9652 | 654 | 7371 | 9302 | 842 | 7606 | 8198 | D411 | 7700 | 8064 |
| 472 | 7840 | 9640 | 660 | 7389 | 9026 | 843 | 7850 | 8212 | D419 | 7176 | 9448 |
| 494 | 7171 | 8292 | 662 | 7541 | 9006 | 851 | 7920 | 8236 | D423 | 7144 | 9508 |
| 505 | 7313 | 8784 | 663 | 7954 | 8964 | 853 | 7873 | 9536 | D425 | 7917 | 9506 |
| 510 | 7288 | 8742 | 664 | 7542 | 9014 | 855 | 7917 | 9532 | D501 | 7956 | 8968 |
| 515 | 7301 | 8732 | 665 | 7604 | 9012 | 860 | 7184 | 8264 | D503 | 7599 | 8962 |
| 520 | 7327 | 8924 | 670 | 7583 | 9274 | 861 | 7920 | 8312 | D516 | 7428 | 9022 |
| 521 | 7326 | 8922 | 690 | 7379 | 9082 | 862 | 7356 | 8260 | D522 | 7542 | 9004 |
| 522 | 7598 | 8918 | 691 | 7367 | 9202 | 863 | 7124 | 8258 | D531 | 7473 | 9306 |
|  |  |  | 692 | 7388 | 9168 | 864 | 7852 | 8256 |  |  |  |

# ACKNOWLEDGEMENTS

My first acknowledgment goes to Kaffe Fassett, without whose inspiration, enthusiasm and support,
I would not have attempted another book.

In the stitching department, a huge thank you goes to Maria Dolores Brannan, for her many hours of
inspired work and for being such a wonderful stitching companion.

Much appreciation and thanks also go to Sarah Windrum. I hadn't worked with Sarah for 20 years and it was a
real pleasure to do so again. Many thanks, too, to David Forrest who braved the ice
and snow and a very cold house to come and stitch for me, and who always does such beautiful work.

Special grateful thanks to June Henry, who runs Kaffe Fassett Designs Limited in Bath, for taking over
the making up of the projects and for producing such wonderful results.

It was a pleasure to meet and work with Su Asher who has painstakingly made such beautiful charts.
My thanks to her.

My appreciation and thanks to Michelle Garrett for her brilliant styling and photography.

Also, once again, thank you to the staff at Paterna for their prompt despatch of yarns and for supporting
me by supplying the wools for this book.

# SUPPLIERS

## UNITED KINGDOM

*KIT SUPPLIERS:*
Jill Gordon Designs,
The Hazels, Hollins Lane, Kingsley,
Staffordshire ST10 2EP;
Tel: 01538 754 712

*YARNS:*
Paterna Yarns,
The Craft Collection Ltd,
PO Box 1, Ossett,
West Yorkshire WF5 9SA;
Tel: 01924 810812

DMC Creative World Limited,
62 Pullman Road, Wigston,
Leicester LE8 2DY;
Tel: 0116 2811040

Coats Paton Crafts,
McMullen Road,
Darlington,
Co Durham DL1 1YQ;
Tel: 01325 381010

*CANVAS:*
William Briggs, School Street,
Bromley Cross, Bolton BL7 9PA;
Tel: 01204 302181

Heebee Design,
27 Willow Green,
Knutsford WA16 6AX;
Tel: 01565 653233

*FIRESCREEN FRAME AND
POPPY SCREEN FRAME:*
David Jackson-Hulme,
Handmade Country Furniture,
Field House Farm, Onecote, Leek,
Staffordshire ST13 7SD;
Tel: 01538 304542

*Different styles of both screens available.*

## UNITED STATES

*KIT SUPPLIERS:*
Susan Merrill Needlework,
10 Story Brook Lane, Amherst,
03031-2604 New Hampshire
Tel: 001 800 955 9911

*YARNS & CANVAS:*
Paternayan, JCA INC,
35 Scales Lane, Townsend,
MA 01469

The DMC Corporation,
Port Kearney Building,
10 South Kearney,
NJ 07032-0650

Coats & Clark,
PO Box 27067, Dept CO1,
Greenville SC 29616

## AUSTRALIA

*KIT SUPPLIERS:*
Ron Mendelsohn, Sunspun
Inspirations, 185 Canterbury Road,
Canterbury, Victoria 3126
Tel: 00 63 9830 1609

*YARNS & CANVAS:*
Stadia Handcrafts,
85 Elizabeth Street, PO Box 495,
Paddington,
NSW 2021

DMC Needlecraft Pty, PO Box 317,
Earlswood 2206, NSW 2204

Coats Patons Crafts, Thistle Street,
Launceston, Tasmania 7250

# INDEX